Photography was Joe Partridge's hobby for years before it became his profession, so he enjoys writing for people who just want to have fun with their cameras.

At the age of 34 he left a career in industry to spend three years at Bournemouth and Poole College of Art studying photography. He now works as a freelance photographer based in London.

He writes on photography for both enthusiast and popular magazines, and broadcasts regularly on LBC's *London Programme* as well as on BBC and other independent radio stations.

He was co-presenter of Yorkshire Television's two popular *Me and My Camera* series, and has written two best selling books on photography.

ONE TOUCH
PHOTOGRAPHY

JOE PARTRIDGE

The Simple Way
to Better
Pictures

Pan Books London and Sydney

For Sally – who thought it was possible

The publishers gratefully acknowledge the assistance of
Nikon (UK) Ltd in the publication of this book.

First published 1984 by Pan Books Ltd,
Cavaye Place, London SW10 9PG
9 8 7 6 5 4 3 2 1
© Joe Partridge 1984
Designed by Fred Price
Line drawings by Ken Smith
ISBN 0 330 28629 3
Printed by Chorley & Pickersgill Ltd Leeds

Contents

Introduction

The trouble with most 'how to do it' photography books is that they take themselves far too seriously. I believe photography should be fun, and I have written this book with that in mind.

The compact autofocus camera has brought about a real revolution in family picture taking. For the first time a simple-to-use completely automatic camera has been coupled with the advantages and range of 35mm film. This means that people can now get excellent results without having to cope with the mass of dials and knobs of more complex cameras.

All the pictures illustrating the book have been taken with autofocus cameras. In many cases they show typical family situations, but some are

deliberately not so: most family photographers won't feel inclined to wait for the sun to rise over a French marsh or use seven dioptres of close-up to take a picture of a flower. But there is very good reason for including these shots; by showing you what the cameras are capable of I hope they will encourage you sometimes to be more adventurous.

'One touch' cameras can truly be called family cameras because they are so easy to load and use that anyone can produce excellent pictures in any situation. So why did I think it necessary to write the book?

During the summers of 1982 and 1983 I toured all over Britain for a major store chain talking to thousands of people about their photographs. Over many weeks I went through their pictures, heard about the problems they experienced, tried to answer their queries and give them helpful tips. *One Touch Photography* has been written with these people in mind

because I know that even with the simplest cameras the pictures you take can sometimes be disappointing, and with a little extra knowledge you can so easily get better results.

There are ten sections in the book and they follow taking a picture step by step from buying the film to putting the prints in the album.

'Getting to know your camera' looks at the parts of a typical camera and explains what they do in more detail than you could ever get from the instructions.

Your camera opens up the wide range of 35mm films to you and 'Getting to know your film' shows you what is available and gives advice on which type to choose for different situations.

'Taking a picture' deals with the practical steps of correctly holding the camera, using the viewfinder and getting the best out of the autofocus system. 'Building the picture' takes a look at what makes a good picture and how to take pictures in the most pleasing way. Also included are some thoughts on how to tackle different lighting situations.

There will be many built-in or additional features to your camera that are new to you and 'More from your camera' explains what these do and how to get the best from them.

'Subjects' looks at all the situations you might want to photograph and offers practical advice on how to make the best of them. From sport to sunsets I will help you choose the right film and the right techniques to produce pictures to be proud of.

Having got your film back from the processors 'Enjoying your pictures' gives advice on getting enlargements, making an album and giving a slide show as well as looking at things that might be wrong with the pictures that were not your fault.

'Looking after your camera' is a small section designed to help you keep your camera in perfect condition so that it will give you years of reliable use.

It is possible that some pictures you take will be less than perfect, and 'What went wrong?' is a quick guide to what caused the problems. At the end of the book there is a glossary that explains some of the words used in photography.

I would like to thank Anne, Les and Terry who helped me with the pictures and I know they enjoyed using the cameras as much as I did. After years of working with the bigger 35mm camera systems I found it really was a delight to go out with a camera small enough to put in my pocket yet able to produce super pictures like those you will see in this book.

Getting to know your camera

Advanced autofocus cameras

Modern autofocus cameras, like the Nikon One Touch cameras, are very easy to use, with automatic loading, focusing, film advance and exposure. Not all cameras will have identical facilities to those described below so you should refer to your instructions.

1. *On/off switch* The cameras are very dependent on battery power and therefore your camera should be switched off when not in use.

2. *Frame counter* Films are available in 12, 24, and 36 exposure cassettes. The counter tells you how many pictures you have taken.

3. *Self-timer* This delays the exposure by ten seconds to let you get in the picture (see page 52).

4. *Film movement indicator* It is important to know that the film is properly loaded and travelling correctly through the camera. This indicator moves as the film does (see page 18).

5. *Film identification window* There is a wide range of film types available for 35mm cameras. Through this window you can identify the type you have loaded.

6. *ASA/ISO setting* Some types of film are more sensitive to light than others. It is necessary to programme the camera with the sensitivity of the film you have loaded (see page 15).

7. *Backlight compensation* In situations where the background is brighter than the subject your picture might be too dark. Pressing this switch will give extra exposure to compensate for this (see page 36).

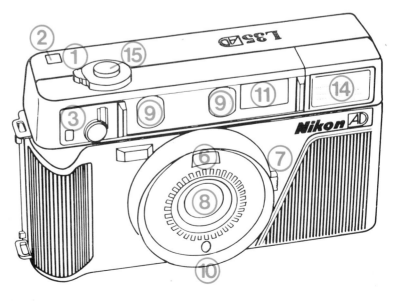

8. *Coated lens* The quality of the lens on modern compact cameras is very high. The coatings are designed to cut down random light that can spoil the picture, but the lens must be kept clean (see page 110).

9. *Focus windows* The autofocus system sends out beams of infra-red light through these windows. Most cameras have several zones to focus in (see page 26).

10. *Exposure window* The brightness of the subject is measured through this window (see page 22).

11. *Viewfinder* As well as assisting you to frame your picture correctly, the viewfinder gives you certain information about focusing and battery life (see page 24).

12. *Tripod socket* It is advisable to support the camera in some low-light situations, and a small tripod screwed to the base is ideal for this (see page 47).

13. *Rewind system* When a 35mm film is finished, it has to be rewound into the cassette before removing from the camera. The camera will do this automatically after you switch on (see page 18).

14. *Flash* The flash will automatically switch on when the light is inadequate (see page 44).

15. *Shutter button* A half-pressure locks the focus with a full pressure taking the picture. If you are using flash, the button will not operate until the flash is ready to use.

16. *Battery chamber* Most compact cameras use easily obtainable AA size batteries to power all the automatic functions (see page 111).

17. *Back release* This opens the back of the camera for loading and unloading the film.

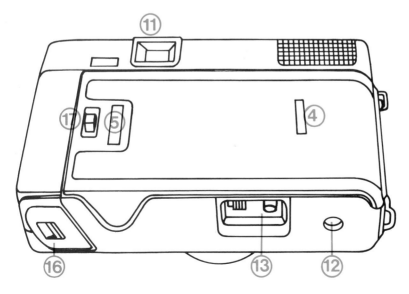

Simple cameras

There are many different autofocus cameras on the market now, some of which are simpler than that shown overleaf. The range of ASA speeds may be limited, confining settings to the popular types of colour negative films. Built-in lens covers are becoming very popular, doubling as on/off switches. Not all cameras have backlight buttons, but you can compensate for this by using the flash (see page 44). The viewfinder may be less sophisticated and there may be a low light warning as opposed to an automatic flash.

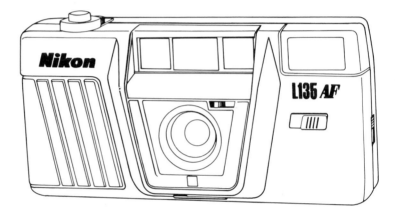

Data back cameras

Data back cameras have the option of printing certain information on to your picture. This will usually be either the year/month/day or the day/hour/minute when the picture was taken. This is useful if you want to catalogue your photographs.

The data back will be powered by its own long-life batteries. The display will blink when they need replacing.

It is important to set your film speed on the back to avoid over-exposing the details.

Getting to know your film

Film types

You will find a wider selection of films available for use in your 35mm compact than for any other popular camera size. The three main types are for colour prints, colour slides or black and white prints, and these are then divided into a wide range of different makes, speeds and uses.

The most popular type is *colour print* film, which produces a negative from which you get colour prints and enlargements. Recent developments have improved the quality of these films enormously and they will give really sharp clear pictures in a wide range of light conditions.

Slide film, called *colour transparency (reversal)* film, is less popular because of problems in showing the slides which you have to project or look at on a battery-powered viewer. You can get prints from colour slides but sometimes they are difficult to obtain and expensive. There are two types of slide film, one for use in daylight or with your flash and one to use with tungsten light sources.

Black and white is less popular than it used to be because processing is expensive and limited to a few outlets.

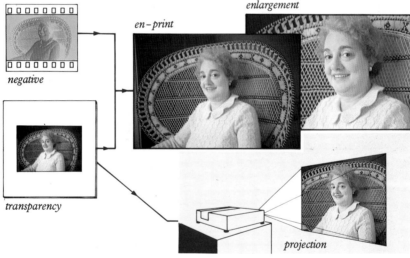

negative

en–print

enlargement

transparency

projection

When buying a film you should read the packet to discover certain important details:

1. *Format* The size you need for your camera is shown as 35mm or 135.

2. *Type* This will show whether the film is for colour prints, slides or black and white.

3. *Speed* This is an indication of the film's sensitivity. The higher the number the less light you need for good pictures.

4. *Number of exposures* Films are available in 12, 24 or 36 exposure lengths, but not all films are available in all three.

5. *Date* Film deteriorates with age and this date indicates the latest time for the film **to be processed.**

Film speed

Film speed is a measure of the film's sensitivity to light. Films with a high speed are more sensitive and need less light to produce a satisfactory picture.

There are three standards for measuring film speed – ASA, ISO or DIN (see pages 124-5). For some time the most popular has been ASA and the film speed dial on your camera will be marked with this. ISO is slowly replacing ASA but since the value is the same you can treat it as ASA. Most film boxes will also show DIN, which is popular in parts of the Continent. Your camera will use different exposures for different speed films so it is important that you set the right film speed. Some cameras have simple sliders with two or three choices; others offer a wide range of settings using a dial. When you are using colour print film it is not so vital to set the exact speed on the camera, but with transparency film you must be absolutely accurate.

Left: In bright light always use a slow or medium speed film.

Right: When taking indoor pictures without flash you should use a fast film.

Slow film 25–50 ASA (ISO) Slow films are normally only available in transparency and black and white, but they will produce the finest quality results. They are only suitable for use in very bright situations.

Medium film 64–200 ASA (ISO) These are the most popular film speeds for most family pictures. Medium film has a good balance between film speed and picture quality.

Fast film 400 ASA (ISO) Use fast film in situations where the light is dull or you want to stop the movement in action subjects. The pictures will be grainier than with slower films.

Extra fast film 1000 ASA (ISO) or more These films are designed for use in conditions where the light is very poor.

The Nikon L35AF has ASA speed settings from 50–1000 ASA. The simpler L135AF has settings for 100, 400 and 1000 ASA.

Film range

When you go into a shop you will be faced with a wide range of film makes, types and exposures. Below are the major brands, grouped by film types and speed.

Different makes of transparency film will vary in colour balance; one make may seem warmer in tone than another. It is worth experimenting with different brands to find one that appeals to you.

colour negative film

colour transparency film (check whether processing is included in price)

black and white film

Choosing a film

When buying a film first ask yourself, 'What do I want it for?' Is it for general use, simply replacing the last film, or is it for a special occasion? The use will very much decide your choice of film speed. For most family and holiday purposes, including winter holidays, a medium speed film with an ASA of 100–200 will be suitable.

Pictures often suffer from the dull light of winter in the UK, and 400 ASA film would be more suitable for that time of year. A faster film also extends the range of your flash so it is ideal for Christmas parties. If you are going to a sports event, or a school play, or if you want to take natural light pictures of a new baby indoors, you would be better buying an extra fast film which will allow you to hand-hold the camera in poor light.

Although they cost more per frame you will often find it better to buy a 12 or 24 exposure film in preference to a 36. For the best quality you should always have your films processed as soon as possible after taking the pictures. Always buy 12 or 24 exposure fast and extra fast films so that you can use them up quickly; they are simply too fast to have in your camera on a bright day.

Because film has a limited life it is better to buy from shops with a rapid turnover where it is well stored. Remember that the date on the film packet is the date *by which the film should be processed*, so think whether you can finish the film in time. Out-of-date films are sometimes offered at discount prices. If they are only just out of date and have been well stored they should give satisfactory results if you use them quickly.

Many people make a 36 exposure film last all year, with the result that the earliest shots lose a lot of quality. It would be much better to buy three 12 exposure films.

A medium speed film should be ideal for your summer holiday pictures.

In dull weather it is better to use a fast or extra fast film.

Loading

You must check that the old film has been rewound before opening the back of the camera. Rewind the film if this has not been done.

When you take the film out you may see that a tab of film remains outside the cassette. This is to help enthusiasts who wish to develop their own film. If you don't want this it is safer to wind the tab back in by turning the knob on the cassette anti-clockwise.

Avoid loading the camera in bright sunlight.

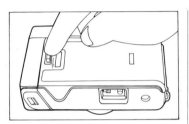

1. Open the camera back.

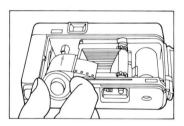

2. Place the film in chamber making sure it engages with the rewind forks. Do not load films where the leader is bent and make sure the film is completely flat before closing the back.

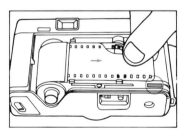

3. Pull the film leader out to the auto loading marks.

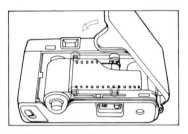

4. Check that the film is properly located in the film guides and close the back.

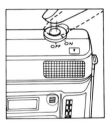

5. Wind on to frame 1 by depressing the shutter button. As you do this, watch the film transport indicator to check the film is travelling correctly.

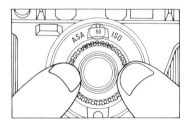

6. Check that the correct ASA is set on the camera.

The sequence above is based on the Nikon L35AF. Other cameras may differ slightly.

Taking a picture

How to hold the camera

The way you hold the camera and stand when taking a picture is one of the most vital parts of getting good results. It is important that you should be comfortable while holding your camera, but there are other considerations.

Holding the camera

Be careful that your hands and fingers do not obstruct any of the working areas on the front of the camera. Obstructing the lens will lead to black marks on your picture; obscuring the flash or exposure measuring windows will spoil the exposure. Anything in front of the autofocus windows will lead to a wrongly focused picture. Most cameras will have grips and pads to help you keep your fingers correctly placed.

This problem is increased when you turn the camera to the vertical format, and you should be especially careful not to cover the flash in this position.

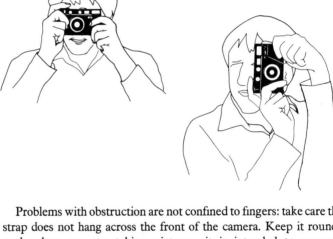

Always stand with your feet apart and your elbows tucked in.

Problems with obstruction are not confined to fingers: take care that the strap does not hang across the front of the camera. Keep it round your neck when you are taking pictures; it is intended to prevent you accidentally dropping the camera.

Supporting the camera

Whenever you take a picture the way you stand is important in getting a sharp image. Stand with your feet apart and your weight evenly distributed. Tuck your elbows into your side and hold the camera firmly against your face.

All cameras have some form of warning when the light is low. Some show a red light in the viewfinder, others automatically activate the flash. This does not mean that you cannot take a picture or must use flash, but that the speed selected is not suitable for hand-holding and that you may get camera shake.

In dull light you can always reduce the risk of camera shake by bracing yourself against a solid object like a tree or a wall.

A more reliable form of camera support is a tripod which will hold the camera steadily at the slowest speeds. The problem is that proper tripods are large and inconvenient to carry around and a better answer would be a pocket mini-tripod. This versatile accessory will hold the camera steadily yet is small enough to carry in your pocket.

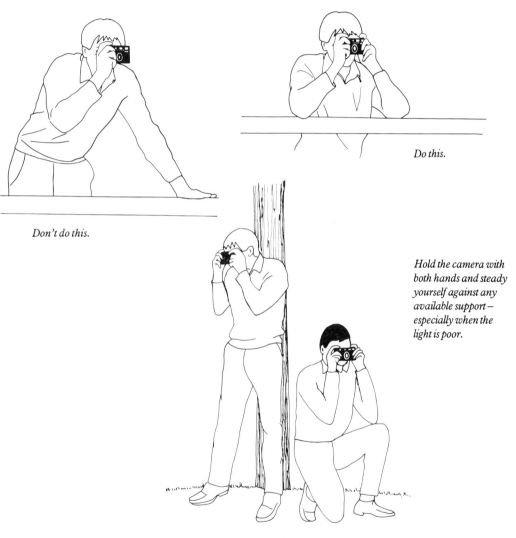

Do this.

Don't do this.

Hold the camera with both hands and steady yourself against any available support – especially when the light is poor.

Pressing the button

All your efforts to hold your camera steady will be to no avail if you jar the camera as you press the shutter release. Always squeeeeeeze the release very gently.

Both the Nikon L35AF and L135AF have sculptured bodies which make them easier to hold. The L35AF is bushed to take a tripod.

21

Exposure and how to control it

When you press the button on your camera, the exposure sensor measures the brightness in front of it and selects the correct exposure – a combination of the aperture and the shutter speed. The aperture is the size of opening the light goes through and the shutter speed is the length of time it is open.

When the weather is bright or you have loaded a faster film, the camera selects faster speeds and smaller apertures. Faster speeds make it easier to 'freeze' action, and smaller apertures give sharper pictures from foreground to background.

The accuracy of the light sensor and the latitude of modern colour print film make it unlikely that you will get a wrongly exposed picture in most situations. But you may get problems when you have a small subject that is considerably brighter or darker than the rest of the picture.

Light subjects

When the subject is much lighter than the rest of the picture it will tend to be over-exposed.

To compensate for this, if possible set a higher film speed on your camera (for example set 200 or 400 with 100 ISO/ASA film). If you cannot do this move closer so that the subject fills a larger proportion of the picture. Remember to return the film speed setting to its normal position afterwards.

Dark subjects

When the subject is darker than the rest of the picture it will tend to be under-exposed.

To solve this problem, with the simplest cameras if possible set a lower film speed on the camera than that of the film you are using. With a 400 ASA film set 100 or 200 but remember to reset it afterwards. Some cameras have a backlight button that does this automatically. An alternative is to use your flash with closer subjects.

Backlight compensation

When the subject is considerably darker than the surroundings or the overall picture is very bright, such as snow scenes, the camera will tend to under-expose, giving you brown, muddy results. Backlight compensation automatically makes allowance for this by giving a longer exposure. In snow scenes this will give you a correct overall exposure but with backlit subjects the background will be over-exposed.

Fill-in flash

An alternative to backlight compensation is to use your flash to brighten up the shadows. The advantage of this is that it will leave the background properly exposed. Because the picture will appear to be lit by two suns there may be a slightly strange look about it, but with practice you will learn the best distance to work at. More sophisticated cameras will balance the value of the daylight with the output of the flash.

If your camera has an automatic flash, simply cover the light sensor in front to activate the flash.

Colour transparencies

There is less latitude with colour slide film and more care should be taken with exposure. You may find that you prefer darker or lighter results and some cameras will allow you to to set slightly slower (to darken) or faster (to lighten) film speeds to adjust this. Try experimenting to find your preference.

The Nikon One Touch L35AF has both a backlight compensation setting as well as automatic daylight flash metering.

Far left: backlit subject

Left: Using backlight compensation

Above: Using fill-in flash

Using the viewfinder

You use the viewfinder of your camera to frame your picture; but it also gives you certain data to help you get better pictures. While some cameras have very simple viewfinders, others give detailed information about focusing.

VIEWFINDER INFORMATION

Whether you have a simple or an advanced camera, you will find taking pictures is very easy, but you do need certain information about focusing and framing. This is displayed in the viewfinder.

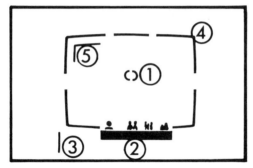

Typical viewfinder

1. *Autofocus frame marks* This is the area that the camera will focus on. In some cameras the focus can be held while you reframe the picture.
2. *Focus symbols* Most cameras focus with a half-pressure on the shutter button when the needle will move across to indicate the zone selected. There are certain situations that will confuse the focus mechanism so you should use the position of the needle as a check. The symbols represent head and shoulders (up to 2 metres/6 feet), waist length (2–3 metres/6–10 feet), full length (3–5 metres/10–15 feet)

and infinity (more than 5 metres/15 feet). Some cameras also have intermediate zones for more precise focusing.
3. *Battery check* The movement of the focus indicator needle shows that the batteries are working properly.
4. *Picture frame indicator* This shows the size and shape of the picture the camera will take.
5. *Parallax compensation marks* These marks are used in preference to the picture frame indicator for framing pictures where the subject is closer than 2 metres/6½ feet.

Different cameras may use all or some of these features, with simpler ones making more use of LEDs, so you should check your own instructions.

The Nikon L35AF has a detailed information viewfinder and the Nikon L135AF has a simple one. The L35AF has seven focus zones, with the four main ones indicated by symbols.

Framing the picture

Bright frame

When you look through the viewfinder you see a 'bright frame' inside it. This represents the size and shape of your picture so you should place your subject within it. Hold your camera close enough to your eye so you can see the whole frame. If you wear spectacles the bright frame will make it easier for you to frame your pictures properly.

Framing for colour prints

If you are using colour print film you should allow a little extra space around your subject within the bright frame. The reason for this is that when the picture is printed the negative is held by a mask slightly smaller than the negative, so if you frame too close to the edge you will lose a little of your picture.

Parallax

If you look at the front of your camera you will see that the viewfinder is placed above, and in some cases slightly to one side of, the lens. This

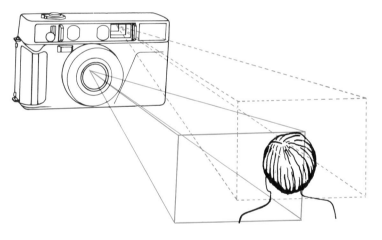

With subjects closer than 2 metres/6½ feet you risk getting a badly framed picture (above) unless you compensate (below).

means that the picture you see through the viewfinder is slightly different from the picture the camera will take. This has little effect with distant subjects but with subjects closer than 2 metres/6½ feet you run the risk of cutting off the top of your subject and need to compensate. Inside the 'bright frame' of more advanced cameras will be part of another frame. When your subject is closer than 2 metres/6½ feet you should use these inner lines to frame your picture.

Simpler cameras have no compensation guides, so with these you should frame close subjects lower in the viewfinder. A spot of bright nail-varnish on the bottom of the viewfinder surround will remind you of this.

The Nikon L35AF has a parallax correction frame.

How the camera focuses

The autofocus system of your camera consists of two windows above the lens and the autofocus frame, a small oblong in the middle of the viewfinder. When you half-press the shutter button a tiny beam of invisible infrared light from the left-hand window bounces back from your subject to the right-hand window. The frame shows you where the beam will strike so it is very important that this is on your subject. The electronics of the camera then measure how long the light took to return and calculate in which zone to set the focus. Some cameras have a scale in the viewfinder to indicate the zone selected, which you can use to verify the accuracy of your focusing.

Most cameras have the facility to lock the focus on a half-pressure of the shutter button which enables you to focus and then compose your picture as you want it. The system is very accurate and will even focus in the dark but there are some situations where care is needed.

When photographing subjects behind glass, the camera may focus on the glass unless you hold it right against the glass or at an angle to it of more than 20°.

If there is a gap between your subjects the camera will not automatically focus correctly. Use the focus lock and reframe the picture to get it right.

Matt black or shiny surfaces like mirrors and water will not reflect the beam properly and may give inaccurate focusing, as will subjects smaller than the autofocus frame. In these situations use the focus lock to focus on an object approximately the same distance away, and then compose your picture.

Both Nikon One Touch cameras have focus locks. The L35AF has seven focusing zones and a minimum focusing distance of 0.8 metres (2 feet 8 inches); the L135AF has 3 zones and a minimum distance of 1.2 metres (4 feet).

Pictures from the TV

Many people want to take pictures of grand occasions or favourite performers from their TV screens. You are not supposed to do this because of copyright but, as long as you only use the pictures privately, it is unlikely anyone will object.

To get good pictures from a TV you need the camera to set a slow shutter speed, so you should use a film with a speed of 100 ASA or less. If the camera is setting a slow speed it will indicate that flash is needed but you *must not* use it. The flash will simply bounce back from the glass screen and spoil your pictures. If your camera has an automatic pop-up flash you should tape it down.

The camera will need to be supported, so either use a tripod or support it on a table using a pile of books to adjust the height at the minimum focusing distance from the screen, remembering to use the parallax compensation marks. Don't set the contrast on your TV too high, and darken the room to cut out reflections from the screen. Press the shutter very gently.

Because of the slow speed set on the camera moving subjects on the TV will be slightly blurred. You will get better results if the subjects are still.

The Nikon L35AF is ideally suited for taking pictures from a TV. It will fit on to a tripod and sets a speed of 1/15th of a second for the brightness of an average TV set.

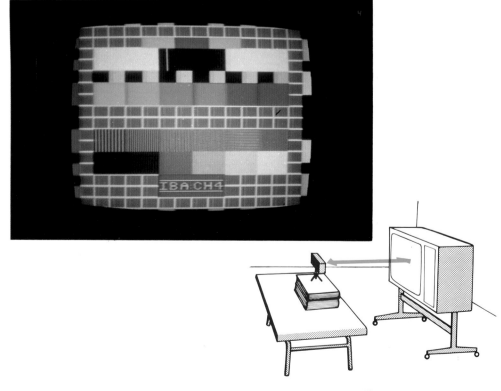

Building your picture

It is as easy to take a good picture as a bad one of the same subject at the same time. The elements that make up the successful picture are simply better arranged. The secret is composition.

Learning a few tricks will help you compose your pictures better. The first question to ask yourself is, Why are you taking the picture? That will help you isolate your subject and concentrate on it. All you then do is to use one or other of the following points to help to improve the way it looks. If you cannot identify the point of interest you should ask yourself whether it is worth taking the picture at all.

Choose your viewpoint

This is one of the most important considerations that should apply to all your pictures. Most of the time you see the world from eye level, so getting lower (a worm's eye view) or higher (a bird's eye view) will give a

By moving closer to this subject and looking up at him the photographer got a much more dramatic picture.

totally different picture. Changing your viewpoint will also help you avoid bad backgrounds and other distractions. Before you take the picture look around to see if you can improve it, by either moving yourself or moving your subject.

Balance the picture (the rule of thirds)

Opposite: the shape of the jetty forms a line that gives depth to this seaside view.

If you imagine your viewfinder divided both horizontally and vertically into three equal parts, and place your subjects on the dividing lines of these thirds, your picture will be more balanced. This will come quite naturally after a little time if you place your subject so it pleases you.

This water garden picture clearly works better in the vertical format.

Change the format

The 35mm camera produces a rectangular picture with the proportions of 3:2. Held in the normal position it gives a horizontal picture that photographers call 'landscape format', but many subjects can be improved if you turn your camera on its side to give a vertical picture. This is called 'portrait format' because it particularly suits pictures of people.

Get in closer

When photographing people a common mistake is to stand too far away. Check the minimum focusing distance of your camera and work your way back from there if you cannot get everything in. Remember that you must allow for the parallax effect of your viewfinder and the processor masking part of your negative, so don't fill the viewfinder frame too tightly.

Leave space

With moving subjects you will increase the feeling of speed if you frame your picture to leave space in front of the subject for it to 'move into'.

The same principles apply to portraits, which will be improved if you leave some space in front of the face for the subject to 'look into'.

Check the background

When looking through the viewfinder it is easy to be so involved with the subject that you forget the background. An untidy background can detract from your picture and a good rule is to 'use it or lose it'. When photographing people be particularly careful to avoid objects like telegraph poles coming out of their heads.

Eliminate distractions

Look out for anything in the picture that distracts from the subject. A very small brightly coloured object in the foreground or background could totally dominate the picture.

Add scale

From babies to landscapes it is useful to include something in your picture that indicates the scale of your subject in its surroundings. The fragility of a tiny baby can be emphasised in your picture by including the father's hands; a high cliff will appear far more impressive if you include a human figure to give it scale.

The tiny human figure indicates just how tall these palm trees are.

Position the horizon

You can change the atmosphere of your picture by the position of the horizon. A low horizon emphasising an interesting sky will give your picture a much airier feel, a high one has the opposite effect. Wherever you put the horizon make sure it is straight!

Use a frame

Many pictures are improved by using a natural object as a frame on one side of the picture. It helps the eye to concentrate on the subject. Trees are useful as frames when photographing views.

The frame formed by the darkened shelter concentrates attention on the girl's face.

Add foreground interest

The slightly wide angle lens of your camera will tend to make things seem more distant in your picture than they look to you. You can counteract this, especially with views, if you include something of interest in the foreground.

Add depth

When photographing a view you will give the picture more depth if you can include something like a road or a wall to lead the eye into it.

Don't be too worried about following all these guides. Like all rules, they are made to be broken; the right picture is the one you like most! Initially it is more important just to get a picture; you can always crop the print to improve the composition before you put it in the album. Remember that better pictures will come with practice.

Before you press the button make sure that you like what you see and, if you don't, do something about it.

Quality of light

The word 'photography' means 'drawing with light', and the quality of the light is the single most important factor in getting good pictures. Light can be roughly categorized as dull, hazy or bright, and each of these has a different effect on your photograph.

Dull overcast weather gives soft shadowless light: cloud cover scatters the sun's rays in all directions and the lack of shadows means that textures (such as wrinkles) become less apparent. Most colours will appear in this light as muted pastel shades, so single strong colours will stand out boldly. The low contrast means that you will see detail all over your picture.

On a hazy day, enough sunlight will come through to give you some modelling without hard shadows, and this is the ideal light for outdoor pictures, especially of people. Because distant objects become indistinct it is less suitable for views unless haziness is the effect you want.

The sharp contrasts of a bright day may mean that you cannot see any details in the shadowed areas of your picture, so be careful how you place your subject. Textured objects like ornate buildings will really stand out when lit from the side.

The strong sunlight of a bright day will emphasise bold primary colours.

Hazy sunshine is the ideal light for outdoor pictures.

Soft lighting gives low contrast so that you see detail all over your picture.

Direction of light

The direction from which the sun hits the subject is very important to the way it will appear in your picture; it gives your subject form through light and shadow. The direction of the light becomes more noticeable as the light strengthens; on an overcast day there are no shadows and the direction is imperceptible.

In the early days of photography the photographer was exhorted to stand with his back to the sun to get the strongest light on his subject. This is called front light and it comes from the direction of the camera. However it is not the ideal light for photographing people: the only shadows on the face will be on the eyes and under the nose, so there will be little modelling. On a bright day it will be uncomfortable for your subjects, who will have to screw up their eyes because of the glare. The lack of shadow with front light will also tend to obscure any texture in the picture, so you will lose much of the charm of, for example, old buildings. When the sun is low in the sky you must also be careful that your own shadow does not get in the picture.

Side light is much better for most pictures because it gives you the shadows that will give shape to your subject. On a very bright day these shadows can be too dramatic and you may need to do something to control the high contrast. Bright hazy days, when the shadows are less extreme, are better for photographing people.

Backlight, when the sun comes towards the camera, can be very dramatic and rewarding but must be treated with care. Make sure especially that the sun does not get into the lens and give you flare. You must also take care with the exposure; your subject is in shadow and will be under-exposed unless you compensate. This can be done either with a backlight button or by using your flash.

Front lighting tends to make your subjects appear flat, with little modelling, whereas side lighting (opposite page, below) gives a more three-dimensional effect.

*Backlight gives a halo
effect. If you fill your
frame with backlit
subjects you will not
need to compensate.*

Time of day/time of year

The quality and colour of light as well as the direction changes throughout the day.

Early in the morning, because the atmosphere is still clear from dust and smoke, the light is crisp with a slight blue cast. The low, weak sun gives long shadows but they are not too dark. You often find that the dawn sky is clear, even when the weather is not good, so it can be worth the effort of getting up to get a special picture.

By noon, when the sun is highest in the sky, the light has hardened. The shadows are at their darkest and pick up a blueness from the sky. You may get problems with the contrast of your pictures and care must be taken with your metering. This is particularly important if your subject is in shadow with a lot of bright surroundings. When it is sunny this is the worst time to take pictures of people.

As the day ends, the light becomes very yellow, bathing everything with a golden glow. With the sun low in the sky the shadows are again very long and you should be careful not to get your own shadow in the picture. In towns and cities look for reflections from high buildings as the golden light strikes the glass walls.

The strength and effect of sunlight very much depend on the sun's height in the sky and will vary as much with the time of year as they do with the time of day. In winter, when the sun is at a low angle, sunlight has to penetrate more atmosphere which diffuses it, giving weak light and long soft shadows.

In the summer, when the sun is at its highest, the light changes with hard light and dark shadows. Spring and autumn offer a compromise between the two, with longer days than winter and a beautiful light, less harsh than in summer.

The different colour and quality of the light at dawn, noon and dusk completely transform this view of Hyde Park.

Colour

The way you see and handle colour will have more effect on the atmosphere of your pictures than any other single factor – the use of colour controls the energy and mood.

To understand how colours react to each other you will find it easier if you think of them as forming a wheel like a rainbow. Those that face each other across the wheel, for example red and blue, are called contrasting

Cool colours come from the blue side of the colour wheel, warm ones from the red side.

colours. If you combine contrasting colours in your pictures you will get a feeling of boldness and activity; but treat them with caution – a little can go a long way. Because they give a strong visual jolt when used together you will often find contrasting colours on signs and flags to attract attention.

Harmonious colours on the other hand are those which are adjacent to each other on the wheel, such as blue and green, and these colours combined will give a more gentle feel to your picture. Similarities of tone and hue mean they go well together, and most of nature's colours come into this category. Harmonious colours can also be created by the colour of the light; the late evening sun casts a golden red over everything.

The colour wheel divides in half to give warm and cool colours. Warm colours are the group on the red side of the wheel, cool colours are the group on the blue side.

Light affects the way you see colours. On a clear sunny day you will find that bright primary colours will appear at full strength, and even in quite small areas they can totally dominate a picture.

On an overcast or misty day, when the soft diffused light takes the bite out of strong colours, you get the opposite effect – muted colours. Your picture seems to be composed of different shades of the same colour, giving lots of mystery and atmosphere. You can artificially mute colours by using cling film over the lens or by slightly over-exposing slide film.

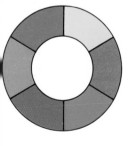

Contrasting colours come from opposite sides of the wheel, harmonious ones are side by side.

Left: Strong primary colours. Below: Muted colours.

41

Artificial light

Most of the pictures you take will be in daylight or using your flash, but from time to time you may be faced with other light sources. The light given off from these may be a different colour from daylight, and will show as a colour cast in your pictures. With colour negative film this cast can be corrected when the prints are made but you must make corrections for transparency film.

Fluorescent light will give your pictures a green cast, but on colour prints this can be improved by the processor.

Ordinary light bulbs (tungsten) will give a yellow cast, but this can often give a picture more atmosphere than you get with flash.

Tungsten light includes domestic light bulbs and theatre lights and will give a yellow cast. You should fit an 80A filter if you are using daylight transparency film, or use a tungsten film. No problems with colour negative film.

Fluorescent tubes and mercury vapour will give a green cast. No problems with negative film; a filter is available for transparency film.

Candlelight will give a warm orange light, but it is better to make no corrections because the colour of the light adds to the atmosphere of the picture.

More from your camera

Flash

The small built-in flash units do not have a great range and you should check your individual instructions for details. It is better to be conservative about the distance. There is absolutely no point in taking flash pictures of anything further away than 5.5 metres (20 feet).

After the 'ready' light comes on wait a few more seconds to make sure the flash is fully charged. As your batteries run down the recycling time will take longer and longer and it is worth carrying a spare set if you expect to take a lot of flash pictures.

Too little flash: take care that your fingers do not obstruct the flash as you take the picture.

Right: Fall off: if you photograph large groups of people using flash the ones at the back will be underlit. Try to arrange them all at an equal distance from the camera.

You will find that your flash will be much more effective in light-coloured rooms than in dark ones, which tend to absorb the light.

Film speed

The range of your flash increases if you are using a fast or extra fast film, so check your camera's instructions for the extended range. Some cameras will indicate the need for flash at the same light value whatever film you have loaded but the table on page 122 will act as a guide to when you ought to use flash with fast film.

Fall off

The light from a flash loses strength over quite short distances, making distant figures appear too dark and close ones too bright. You will get better pictures if you group your subjects all at the same distance from the camera.

Reflections

The flash will bounce back from any glass or shiny surface directly in front of you and spoil your picture. Either move your subject or position yourself so that you are at an angle to the problem surface.

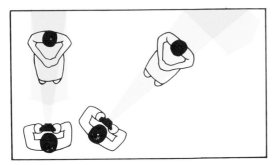

Take care that reflections do not spoil your flash pictures.

Remember that you can use your flash in daytime, when your subject is in shadow.

Red eye

If your subject is looking straight at the camera in a dark room there is a danger that the light will reflect from the back of their eyes giving them a red appearance. To avoid this, try to increase the room lighting and get your subject to look slightly away from the camera.

The built-in flash on your camera is very versatile but not very powerful. You will always get much better flash pictures if you take them with the subject 1.8–2.8 metres (6–9 feet) away.

The flash on the Nikon One Touch L35AF has a range of up to 3.6 metres (11.8 feet) with 100 ASA film.

45

Winder

Most autofocus compact cameras will automatically wind on after each picture, recocking the camera ready for the next shot. With fresh batteries this takes about a second.

The big advantage of this is that you don't have to take the camera away from your eye to wind it on after each picture; consequently you are able to concentrate more on the subject. This is particularly useful when you are photographing mobile subjects such as children playing. You and the camera are always ready for the unexpected.

With the help of the winder in your auto-focus camera you are always ready for the unexpected.

People often tense up when they see a camera, only relaxing after the picture has been taken. With the winder the camera will automatically be ready to take the better second picture. Don't try this when you are using flash; it is likely that the flash will take several seconds longer to recharge.

If you are photographing a group where you know that extra pictures will be required, it is easy, with the automatic advance, to take extra pictures which will be considerably cheaper than reprints.

But always treat the automatic advance facility with caution; it is easy to get carried away and take unwanted pictures.

The same mechanism in the camera rewinds the film when you have taken all the pictures. This is normally a two-part process, firstly disconnecting the forward mechanism and then activating the rewind motor. Cameras differ and you should consult your leaflet.

Both the Nikon One Touch cameras have automatic film advance and rewind.

Tripods

In poor light conditions your camera will select a slow shutter speed. It normally warns you of this by activating either the flash or the low light warning. But it is neither desirable nor possible to use the flash in every low light situation. Your subject may be out of range, or you may want to use the longer exposure to catch a night-time scene or the blur of action.

When the camera has selected a slow speed it is impossible to hold it steadily by hand. At anything slower than 1/60th of a second the slightest movement of the camera will cause blur. At some speeds this will not be

The legs of a mini-tripod fold up and fit inside the body.

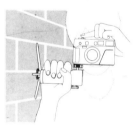

obvious on enprints, only manifesting itself on enlargements, but at its worst the picture will be unusable.

In these situations you will need to support the camera, and a tripod is the most efficient way of doing this. Many cameras have a threaded socket in the base specially for fixing them to a tripod.

There are two types of tripod. Professional and enthusiast photographers use large ones which are very versatile but expensive and bulky to carry around. Mini-tripods on the other hand are low priced and will easily fit into your pocket. With a little imagination they can be as versatile as their big brothers. While they do not have the height of a big tripod, you can usually find something like a rock or the bonnet of a car to place them on. Equally you can use them on their side and brace them against a wall or pillar.

The Nikon L35AF has got a tripod thread.

A mini-tripod can be used to brace the camera against the wall.

47

Filters

The more sophisticated compact cameras have a screw thread in front of the lens that can be used to mount threaded glass filters. Some filters are used to change the colour of the light reaching the film to correct colour casts, while others add special effects. A further range allows you to get much closer to your subject (see page 52).

Most filters will affect the exposure, but as long as the filter also covers the sensor the camera will compensate automatically.

Ultra-violet filter

The main purpose of an ultra-violet (u/v) filter is to remove excesses of ultra-violet light which may add a blue cast to your pictures, especially on clear days and in high locations. An added benefit is that it will protect the lens from damage.

Polarising

It may be tricky to use a polarising filter on your camera but you will find it worthwhile. It has two uses – controlling reflections and putting the blue back in skies. The problem is that the position of the filter is critical to get the best effect. Hold the filter to your eye and rotate it until you get the effect you want. Note the position of the white spot on the filter in relation to your picture and, having screwed the filter on the camera, rotate it until the spot is in the same position.

A starburst filter can add a magical quality to a nighttime scene.

Starburst

A starburst filter has the effect of turning points of light into stars. They are available to give 4, 6 or 8 point stars and are particularly effective in night shots or with Christmas tree and street lights.

Correction

Correction filters are used to change the colour of light and are more necessary when you use colour transparency film than with colour negative, which can be corrected during printing. An 80A filter removes the yellow cast when daylight film is used in tungsten light.

81A or 81B filters are used to make colours warmer, especially during winter.

A wide range of filters are available commercially but you can also improvise your own. To get a soft effect for portrait pictures you can cover the lens with kitchen clingfilm; and by holding a toffee paper halfway down the lens you can add colour to a dull sky. Make sure you don't block the autofocus at the same time!

The Nikon L35AF is threaded for 46mm filters.

A polarising filter can be used to cut out reflections.

A toffee paper was used to create this dramatic sky.

49

Close-ups

It is possible to take exciting close-ups with some of the more sophisticated compact cameras because supplementary close-up lenses will screw on the front of the lens. There are four strengths measured in dioptres: +1, +2, +3 and +4; you can use two together to give a maximum strength of +7.

Each close-up lens gives revised distances to the subject for the different focus settings on a camera. Because your camera is autofocus it is safest to calculate on its closest focusing distance, getting it to focus there

Above: this is the closest you could get to a flower without using supplementary lenses.

Right: the same flower photographed using +2, +4 and opposite, +7.

by holding a marker card just in front and using the self-timer to lock the focus. To keep the camera steady it should be on a tripod.

Accuracy is critical, so it is worth experimenting. You may get disappointing results with moving subjects like animals or flowers on a windy day. If you are likely to take a lot of close-up pictures, it will be worth building a small stand to hold the subject at the correct distance from the camera.

You will get better results in bright, overcast daylight using reflectors to fill in the shadows. With close-ups, especially on a dull day, only a limited amount in front and behind your subject will be in focus, so flatter subjects are better.

The problem of parallax is increased in close-up photography, so you will need to line up the subject and **lens** by eye rather than through the viewfinder.

The Nikon L35AF takes 46mm screw thread close-up lenses.

Cut a marker card to match the focal length of the close-up lens you are using. Use this to position the camera correctly in relation to the subject, lock the focus and remove the card before taking the picture.

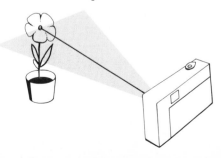

Self-timer

One of the saddest aspects of family pictures is that the group is often incomplete. After all, someone had to take the picture. The more sophisticated autofocus cameras have a self-timer which, used properly, will help get you all in the shot.

Set up the group, say at a café table, being careful to leave an easily accessible place for yourself. You will obviously need to support the camera. Often some books on another table will suffice, but a pocket tripod would be ideal. Switch on the timer and frame your shot, making

With your self-timer switch you can either include yourself in family groups or take unusual self portraits.

sure that the autofocus frame is on one of the group. Now gently push the button: the focus is locked as soon as you do this and with most cameras you have around ten seconds to get to your place. The warning light will flash for the last three seconds so that you can compose yourself.

With most cameras the self-timer will have to be switched off afterwards, which is easily done by returning it to its normal position.

Because the self-timer electronically activates the shutter, it is useful for taking pictures where the camera is on a tripod and should not be jarred. Set up the shot normally and simply activate the timer. But remember that the ten-second delay makes this method impractical for action subjects.

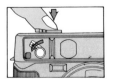

The Nikon L35AF has a ten-second self-timer.

52

Subjects

Family

We photograph our families and friends more than any other subject, but sadly the results are often disappointing. By following a few basic tips your results can be improved beyond recognition.

Take your time! Surprisingly one of the biggest problems with family pictures is familiarity: when looking through the viewfinder, you see only your subject and forget to check the rest of the frame. The result is that the overall look of the pictures is often untidy. Before pressing the button allow your eye to look round the viewfinder to check for distractions.

If there are distractions the easiest remedy is to change your viewpoint. You will often find that simply moving a few steps to one side will solve the problem. This careful selection of your viewpoint also applies to your height in relation to the subject. Getting down on your knees or up on a chair will give you a totally different picture.

Get as close as you can to your subjects and try to catch them when they are absorbed in one another.

It is faces that friends want to see, and if you stand too far back the subject will be too small to recognize. Get in as close as practical and fill the frame – being careful to correct your framing so that you don't cut off the top of someone's head. Use a little caution with single faces; the slightly wide angle lens of your camera may distort the face if you are too close.

There is a big exception to the rule about getting closer. One of the most interesting things about looking through an album is to see where people

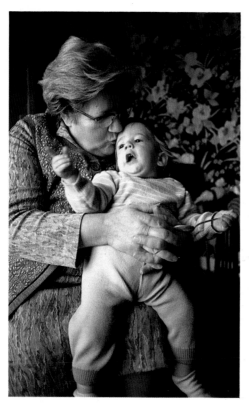

lived and the clothes they wore. Include your home in some pictures. These shots are especially good for making Christmas cards or when writing to distant friends.

Candid shots when the family are playing or talking together will often give you a better picture than a formally posed group.

Instead of lining everyone up for the posed picture try a 'candid' shot – even if you have to pose it! When all the family are doing something together it will avoid the woodenness of a formal picture. Meal times or playing board games together are the kinds of activity that work well.

With occasions like Christmas or holidays, photograph the preparations as well as the event. The chaos of packing is as much part of the holiday atmosphere as anything else.

If the family have gathered for a birthday or anniversary, first position the main subject and then group the rest of the family around them. It is always worth taking several pictures of events like these. Other people are bound to want copies, and originals are cheaper than reprints. It will also be insurance against someone closing their eyes at the moment you take the picture.

The quality of modern fast films makes it possible to take pictures indoors in daylight without flash. It may be necessary to position your subject near a window but the results will be worth the trouble. Extra fast film will even allow you to take pictures with bright room lights, but buy a 12 exposure and use it up quickly because it could be too fast for outside use.

0.8 metre (2 feet 8 inches) is the closest you can go with the Nikon L35AF and 1.2 metres (3 feet 10 inches) with the L135AF.

Babies and children

Your autofocus compact is the ideal camera for photographing babies and children. The autofocus and automatic exposure will give you fast sharp pictures and the built-in winder means that the camera is always ready.

Opportunities for good photographs of babies and young children happen very quickly. Make sure that all the family can use the camera – keep it loaded and accessible all the time. The rules about background and composition obviously apply to all pictures, but with babies and children the first priority is to get a picture of some sort. Unless you are confident of your technique don't waste time trying to arrange a picture, because the moment will pass.

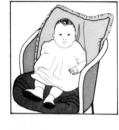

Choose your viewpoint carefully when photographing children. It is better to go down to their level; pointing the camera down results in a distorted and unnatural pose. With babies in their cots the bedding will act as a natural reflector but once they are twelve weeks old, support them in a chair and get someone alongside you to attract their attention.

Use your camera to keep a record of a baby's daily life.

Put a new toy in the place where you want to take your photograph.

Bath time, feeding and when they are sleeping are ideal opportunities to take pictures of happy babies, but don't forget that tears are part of their character as well.

Even indoors you should use daylight in preference to flash whenever possible. Modern fast films make this quite easy and the softer light is more pleasing. Move a cot or a playpen close to a window to make the best of this light. Photographing young children indoors is the ideal time to use extra fast film.

Babies will appear quite small in your viewfinder, so be careful not to get closer than your camera will focus. As they get older they may become self-conscious and you may need to go even further back, but you can always crop the picture afterwards.

As children grow older, you will find that candid pictures have more charm. Place new toys in positions where the light suits you; as they become engrossed in the toys you will have an ideal picture opportunity.

With a new baby, make it a rule to take a picture every week: they grow so quickly. If you take it in the same place you will have a reference to show how much they have grown. Take more pictures than you normally would; you can always send duplicates to grandparents and friends.

If you set up a picture, remember that children will get bored after a short time. Don't try to force the situation if there is any awkwardness, but leave them and go back another time.

Keep your camera ready to catch special moments.

Portraits and groups

An informal portrait is often the best way to capture personality.

The lens of your autofocus camera is not really suitable to do a full-face portrait because you might get some distortion. Move back a little and take either a half-length or the whole figure. With a little care this will make a charming picture and you have the option to crop closer on the print.

But this does not mean that you have to have your subject standing like a sentry staring straight at the camera. Most people, unless they have been photographed a lot, get very self-conscious in front of a camera, and if you arrange for them to be doing something you will get a much more natural picture. Painting and reading are excellent because the paper will act as a reflector and throw light back into your subject's face.

If you have two people in your picture, get them to look at each other. This will improve the composition and show the bond between your subjects.

Try to keep your backgrounds simple. A little time either choosing an uncluttered location or moving any distractions will give you a much better picture.

The wide angle lens, although it can be a slight problem with individual portraits, becomes a positive advantage with groups. It means you do not have to go too far back to get everyone in. Make sure that you can see everyone. If you are photographing a large group you may need to pose them on stairs or at different levels.

With a large group you want to be able to attract everyone's attention at the right moment. Unless you have a very loud voice you might need some artificial help. A referee's whistle is ideal.

If you are going to do a family group you should find a large chair is sufficient to build your group around. Remember to include any family pets, who are as much part of the family as anyone else. This is the time to use the self-timer so that you can be in the picture. Set up the group, leaving an accessible place for yourself with the camera supported or on a tripod. Frame your picture and then, having focused and activated the timer, simply get into position.

For a group picture try to arrange your subjects at different heights to make an interesting composition.

Rather than using flash to take portraits indoors make your own reflector with a piece of white card.

If you are taking a little time to get a good picture it is worth paying special attention to the light. The output of your flash is limited and, with its hard direct light, is a little harsh, so try to use daylight whenever possible. With modern films this should be possible on all but the dullest days. Position your subject by a window to get the best light and then use a reflector to lighten the shadows. Anything white or silver will do but a sheet of card that can be propped on a chair will be best.

Some old people are very self-conscious about the lines on their faces. If this is the case you will find the gentle light of a dull day will soften the texture. You could also use a diffusing filter to get the same effect.

Pets

The problems and techniques of photographing pets are very similar to those of photographing children. The art is getting them to stay still long enough in the right place. The easiest way of doing this is simply to include them with other members of the family: in a family group, sitting with someone in a chair or playing outside with a child.

The choice of background and viewpoint is important: there is no need to prepare special backgrounds but make sure that there are no distracting elements. Rather than trying to get your pet to where you want to take the picture it is better to go to him, as most pets are creatures of habit and you will know where his favourite sitting or sleeping spots are. You can prepare the spot beforehand by tidying up the background and arranging furniture. When choosing your viewpoint it is usually better to get down to the pet's level.

The big advantage of your autofocus compact camera is that it is always ready to take pictures, which will enable you to take advantage of funny situations your pet gets involved in. The closer you get to a subject the more accurate your focusing must be, so always focus on the animal's face.

Pets are part of the family: it is often best to take pictures of them with their owners.

Get someone to hold a small pet like a hamster so that you can take your picture and then crop it.

Do not use flash if you can help it. Most animals' eyes will show up as red in flash pictures if they are looking towards you and the harsh light and shadows is not very attractive. The latest extra fast films will allow you to take pictures indoors in daylight.

Your camera will select a faster shutter speed on a bright day or when you have loaded a faster film; you will need this faster speed if your pet is very lively. This might even apply if he is being held, because a fast movement of the head could result in blur.

Dogs are the most obliging pets to photograph. Because they are bigger it is easier to fill the frame, and if they are obedient you can actually 'pose' them. Photographing dogs is easiest just after they have eaten but with younger dogs, who lose their concentration quickly, you still have to be very quick. Try to photograph dogs out of doors where they will look more natural.

Cats look more at home indoors but, as any cat owner knows, you cannot make them do anything they do not want to do so you have to tempt them. A hot water bottle placed under a rug will usually keep them in that spot and then, when you are ready to take the picture, you can make a noise to get them to look at the camera. Because they are relatively small you must be careful not to get closer than your camera can focus; take your picture from the minimum recommended distance and have an enlargement made for the album.

The obvious problem with small pets like hamsters or mice is also getting close enough. Even at the minimum recommended distance they will appear very small in the viewfinder and you may not be able to get them accurately in focus. They are also very active, so the best solution is to get someone to hold them in his hands. This is another situation where you will need to crop an enlargement for a really successful picture.

Weddings and parties

Your camera is ideal for special occasions like weddings because it is small enough to fit in a bag or pocket and it will be instantly ready for a picture. It is a good idea to use a fast film which will be suitable for taking pictures both in and out of doors as well as extending the range of your flash.

There is usually an official photographer at a wedding and there is no point in taking pictures over his shoulder that merely duplicate his efforts. But the professional usually arrives at the church and leaves early from the reception which gives you lots of scope for pictures both before and after and relaxed informal shots whilst they are there.

Unlike the official photographer, you may be able to catch the excitement and the intimate family moments before the wedding starts. You may also get some views that the official photographer never saw.

Begin with some shots of the bride at home. Make sure you don't get in the way – people may be feeling quite tense already. But you may be able to record some intimate moments between the bride and her parents.

If you are allowed to take pictures in the church you will need to use the available light because your flash is not suitable. Support the camera with a mini-tripod and use the self-timer to trigger it.

Outside the church and at the reception look for the candid situations that will say so much more about the day than the professional's pictures. He will have left after setting up a picture of the cake cutting, so you have the chance to capture both the intimate and funny moments that develop during the speeches and toasts.

At any party it is better to pose groups of friends quite informally rather than just snap away. It will only take a couple of seconds to get a group together, and there will be less danger of misfocusing through a gap.

A smoky atmosphere will reduce the effectiveness of your flash and in this case you should go a little closer than usual. If you are photographing a group sitting at a table remember that the fall-off of the flash will give you uneven lighting, with the foreground light and the background dark. You will get a better picture if you can group everyone at about the same distance away from you round the guest of honour at one end. It may still help to use fast film and available light rather than flash. Standing up on a chair and shooting down will give you a more interesting viewpoint.

Concerts and occasions

Concerts

You must be careful about using your camera at concerts and similar events. Often photography is forbidden, and even if it is not, the use of flash may disturb both the audience and the performer. Unless you are in the very front there is no point in using your flash anyway: the range is very limited.

The meter of your camera will be able to cope with the stage lighting if you are close enough for it to fill the viewfinder, but you will get problems if you are some distance away because of the large area of black around the well-lit stage. If this is the case set the camera to twice the ASA speed of the film you are using.

If you are close to the stage it is best to use a fast or extra fast film as many modern performers move around a lot and you will need the speed to freeze any action. Don't use the camera during any really fast parts because you will still get blur; it is better to wait for the 'peak of the action' (see page 80).

If you are in a crowd be careful with your framing. Because of the 'parallax' effect you may be able to see an uninterrupted view through the

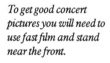

To get good concert pictures you will need to use fast film and stand near the front.

viewfinder while the lens is 'seeing' the top of the heads in front. You can of course reverse this effect by turning the camera upside down.

The lighting is most likely to be tungsten, which gives a yellow cast. This can be corrected at the printing stage if you are using colour print film but you should warn the processor. With transparencies you will need to use a film designed for that type of lighting.

Circus acts

The same principles apply as for concerts except that there is usually no restraint on using cameras. A seat at the front will be an advantage as will fast film. Wait for a natural pause in the action to take your pictures to avoid blur.

Plays

It is totally forbidden to use a camera at professional stage productions and at most amateur and school productions as well. If you are allowed to take pictures of a play, the problems will be similar to those at concerts. You will get much better pictures if you can arrange to attend a dress rehearsal, when you will be able to work on the stage and fill your frame with the actors and the set. This is what the professional theatre photographers do and it has the added advantage that you will be able to get detail shots.

Left: Look out for colourful characters in the carnival parade rather than general views where they may get lost in the crowd.

Public occasions

The position you get at public occasions is vital to good pictures and the only way to guarantee this is by getting there first and securing a good place. A high viewpoint will be ideal for watching but the subject will appear rather small in your pictures because of the coverage of the lens.

If you are blocked in by the crowd try holding the camera above your head, pointing in the direction of the subject, and taking a chance with a few pictures. If you are lucky the autofocus will set itself properly and your pictures may even show more than you were able to see.

Right: You might have problems with fire eaters as your camera will not focus properly on flames. Use a substitute subject to focus on and then use your focus lock while you reframe the picture.

*Opposite: Look for
an unusual angle
on a familiar
landmark.*

Holidays

The joy of holiday pictures is that on a winter's night, months after the tan has faded, they help you to relive the excitement. But if you don't want the camera to dominate your holiday you'll need to feel confident about how to use it.

Before you go

Always try out a new camera before going away. It will help you to get used to it before you want to take those once in a lifetime pictures. Use a 12 exposure film and get it developed before you go.

It is always worth insuring your camera. A household 'all risks' policy is ideal but this may not automatically cover you if you are abroad, so let your insurance company know.

*Some of the most
striking and unusual
views may be of
everyday objects.*

It is a good idea to take your film with you; while most of the popular makes of film are available worldwide you might not be able to buy your favourite brand. All airports use x-ray security checks on hand baggage, so keep your film in your pocket and ask for it to be hand checked. Remember to do this on your return as well.

To avoid exposure problems when photographing stained glass windows get in close and fill your viewfinder.

Although most of your pictures will hopefully be in sunshine when you can use slow or medium film, it is worth taking a short roll of extra fast film for overcast days or interior shots. In many much-visited buildings, such as the Vatican's Sistine Chapel, you are allowed to take pictures but you must not use a tripod or flash; an extra fast film could help you get pictures in these situations.

If you do need to buy a film abroad, choose it carefully. Avoid buying films that are unfamiliar: in some countries it is difficult even to decipher what type of film it is from the box.

Unless you are really going off the beaten track, AA size batteries should be readily available; but don't forget that you are likely to take more flash pictures on holiday which will use up power faster. If you do take batteries with you make sure they are properly packed: they will lose power if the terminals touch each other.

Don't forget to pack your cleaning kit. In dry dusty conditions you should clean the camera frequently. With all the family using the camera there is also a greater chance of getting marks on the lens and exposure-measuring window; these must be clean to give you the best results.

Don't forget that the holiday really begins before you leave home. Pictures of the preparations can make an interesting start to the album or a slide show.

Taking pictures on the move

It is not easy to take good pictures from moving vehicles, whether planes, trains or coaches. The glass windows will confuse the autofocus and may set up reflections, and the vibration may cause camera shake. Choose a position where you are both comfortable and stable; you cannot be really steady if you have to lean across other people. Hold the camera against the glass or at an angle of more than 20°, and lock the focus. If possible check the focus setting has reached the required symbol. The double windows of planes are particularly tricky. You will need to get close to the window to cut out background reflections. Do not hold the camera against the glass when you take the picture because you will pick up too much vibration from the engine.

It is possible if you take great care to get clear shots on the move from aeroplanes, buses or trains.

Look ahead to see if there are any obstructions coming: you don't want a picture of the inside of a tunnel. For the same reason concentrate on objects in the distance for your picture. Anything in the foreground will be blurred because of the speed at which you are moving.

Photography, including pictures from the plane, is forbidden in many airports, so be careful to follow any instructions.

If you are travelling by car make sure your camera and film don't get too hot, as this can spoil pictures. The glove compartment and the back ledge are particularly bad in this respect. Remember to keep your camera out of sight if you are leaving the car; a thief needs only a few seconds to break in.

Pictures in the sun

In bright sunny locations your biggest problem will be with contrast. This is the difference between the bright areas of your picture and the shadow areas. In a situation of average brightness where there is a balance between

Get in as close as possible for good beach pictures.

brightness and shadows the camera will give you a correct exposure, but the problems arise if either is too dominant. When photographing people on a very bright beach, use the backlight button to compensate unless you are very close or they will be under-exposed. Alternatively you can use the flash to fill in the shadows (see page 22).

The harsh bright light of noon is not the best light for taking pictures because of the very black shadows. It will be more comfortable to take pictures and you will get better results in the softer light earlier or later in the day.

If your camera will take filters it is worth keeping a u/v on all the time in sunny weather. Clear blue skies give an increase in ultra-violet light that without the filter can make your pictures slightly blue. The added advantage is that the filter will protect your lens from damage.

If you are taking pictures into the sun you may need to shield your lens to avoid flare. You can do this with your hand, but hold it above and well away from the camera to make sure you don't either block the focus mechanism or get your hand into the picture.

If you take your camera on the beach be sure to keep it in a bag away from the sand. It is a precision tool and any sand in it could cause damage. Keep the camera in the shade as the hot sun could spoil the film.

You must protect the camera from salt water, wiping off any splashes immediately with a cloth dampened in fresh water. If you have the bad luck to drop the camera into the sea you should immediately immerse it in fresh water and quickly get it to a qualified repairer.

Winter holidays

The brilliant light on a sunny day in winter resorts can cause problems with exposure: the camera senses the brightness and under-exposes the picture, resulting in grey snow! If your camera has a backlight compensation you can use this to give the extra exposure. If not, set the film speed indicator to a lower speed, for example set 400 ASA film at 100 ASA, and this will compensate. (If you do this remember to reset the original speed afterwards). If you are photographing people outside it will be better if you get close. If you fill the viewfinder you will not need to compensate for the exposure.

Right: when taking pictures in the snow you may have problems with under-exposure. One solution is to fill your viewfinder.

Opposite: colourful street scenes will capture the flavour of your holiday.

If you are taking pictures of the local people make sure first that they have no objections.

If you have been outside in the cold taking pictures and then return to a warm interior you will get condensation on the camera. Not only will this make it impossible to take pictures until it has cleared, but it is not good for the camera. Put the camera in a plastic bag and seal it. It will then return to room temperature gradually and will be condensation free.

To photograph moving skiers you will need to use the panning technique illustrated on page 80 to freeze the action.

The mountain air is very clear and there is an increase in ultra-violet light which may make your pictures look a little blue. If your camera will take filters a u/v will compensate for this and protect the lens at the same time.

People and towns

Many people use postcards to help select a viewpoint for photographing landmarks when they arrive in a new place; but it is more fun to put the postcards in your album and look for a different view for your own pictures.

Pictures of the buildings in foreign towns and villages are an important part of any holiday album, and the wide angle lens on your camera will help you to get more in. But if you point the camera up the buildings will appear pointed. You can get over this by moving further back and using part of the picture (see page 85), or by climbing higher so that you don't have to point the camera up at such a steep angle.

Because of your wide angle lens you will have to get relatively close to take portrait shots. Many people don't like having their pictures taken, and in some countries it is officially frowned upon. To avoid embarrass-

ment the simplest thing to do is to point to your camera and to the person to indicate that you would like to take pictures. This is particularly important with members of the police and armed forces.

In some countries it has become customary for people to ask for money for posing. It is a personal matter what you do about this and if you are on a tour your guide will advise you.

There is more to the life in foreign countries than the people and the grand buildings. Look for the small details that show the difference between their life and your own.

In some places abroad, particularly airports, you may need to get official permission to take photographs.

When travelling abroad look out for the details of everyday life that will lend local colour to your pictures.

General advice

When you are taking holiday pictures, be especially careful to identify your point of interest and take a little time to build your picture around it. There is always a temptation to take pictures of everything you see; resist this because it results in too many disappointing and costly failures.

Carry your camera with you at all times; it is small enough to fit in a bag or belt pouch. Not only is it more secure with you than in your hotel room but if you have not got it with you you are bound to see something you want to photograph.

If you see something you like resist the temptation to leave the picture until another day. Weather is so changeable it may never look the same.

Take your camera out at night too so that you can record those delicious exotic meals.

When you go out in the evening, carry a spare set of batteries. You will use the flash a lot and it is very frustrating if you run out of power in the middle of a party. Don't forget that original prints are cheaper than reprints; if you are with friends, take two pictures so you have one to send to them.

In most parts of the world there are areas where photography is forbidden. It is silly to break the rules because it could lead to serious problems with the authorities. If there is any doubt ask the advice of your courier or hotel proprietor. Transport facilities, which may serve both military and civil needs, are often subject to this type of restriction.

There is so much happening in many street scenes that your pictures may become cluttered. Go in closer and concentrate on the detail that can say as much about the way people live as the general view. Street and town names on signs and posters can be used as titles in albums or slide shows.

If you intend to make an album when you get home it will be fun to collect other items to put alongside the pictures. Menus and tickets will add an extra dimension, as well as postcards to supplement your own pictures.

Sunsets

It is worth taking several shots of a sunset in rapid succession as the light changes very quickly. Anything in the foreground will appear in silhouette.

Once the sun starts to set you should not waste any time getting ready to take your pictures – it will vanish all too quickly. The colours and shapes will change so rapidly, you may want to take several shots to get different effects.

You should not need to support the camera until the sun reaches the horizon, when the strength of the light decreases very quickly. If you don't have a tripod put the camera on the edge of a table and use the self-timer to fire it.

If you are using transparency film you can vary the exposure by setting an ASA speed twice that of the film in the camera. You do not need to do this with colour print film.

Because the meter will react to the bright sunset, anything in the foreground will appear in silhouette. Position yourself so you can use this effect to frame your picture. The focusing mechanism might be confused by the bright sun, so focus to one side and use the focus lock.

Landscapes and views

There always seems to be a difference between your memories of a view and your pictures. The problem is that your eye takes the broad view and merges all the aspects, automatically discarding distractions and compensating for contrast in lighting. The camera, on the other hand, faithfully records what is in front of it.

Start by asking yourself what is it that appeals to you. This will help you choose one element of the scene to put the emphasis on as you compose your picture.

The greatest challenge with a view is to give it depth. You can do this by using foreground interest or a 'frame', such as a tree, which will also draw the viewer into the picture. You can use roads, walls or paths to lead the eye into the picture and also lend perspective, which is another aid in achieving depth. You may find that moving your viewpoint, often only a

Foreground interest and the frame of the tree branches lead the eye into this long-distance lakeside view.

High up on a snowy mountain where the air is very clear you should get a fine sense of perspective.

few metres, will enable you to strengthen your composition and avoid distractions like power lines or bright notices.

Be sure to hold your camera so you get a straight horizon, and think about its position in the picture. A high horizon emphasises depth, a low one gives a feeling of airiness.

Because of the scale of a landscape the quality and direction of the light are critical. If the important areas are in shadow it will be better to take the picture later, when the sun is in a different position.

An ultra-violet filter will reduce the amount of haze in the distance, or a polarising filter will strengthen all the colours.

Panoramas

The delight of a panorama is that it enables you to record a view that is too big for your camera; for example, you can make a 360° panorama of the view from the peak of a mountain. You want the individual prints to match, so try to keep your camera level and the focusing the same. Because of the different perspective of objects close to you it will be better to keep any foreground interest to a minimum. Overlap the pictures you take by at least a half; you will find this easier to calculate if you select some points in the view for references. Ask the processor to try to match the exposures of the prints.

When you get your pictures back lay them out overlapping and, using a sharp knife and a steel ruler, cut the top one in the middle of the overlap, then re-align and cut the bottom one to match it. Then either paste them into your album or tape them together on the backs.

Sport and action

It would be fair to say that the autofocus camera is not ideal for taking sports pictures. You will often find that the image in the viewfinder is simply not big enough to make an acceptable picture because you cannot get close enough. The range of the flash will be a limitation at indoor sporting events for the same reasons. Finally, since you have little control of the shutter speed selected by the camera, you cannot be sure of freezing fast action. The top sports photographers will use a wide range of cameras, lenses and other sophisticated equipment as well as having the pick of the locations, so there is no point in trying to compete with them.

Nevertheless there are many opportunities where, with care, you can produce super pictures. The subjects for an action photograph can be anything from a downhill ski racer to a child on a tricycle, yet the principles for a successful picture are the same. Timing; position; technique: these are the three keys to successful action photography.

One big advantage you have is that your camera is autofocus; if you aim it correctly it will focus on a moving subject in the fraction of a second as the picture is taken. Fast focusing is vital for good action pictures.

At many sporting events you are unable to move around freely so the position you sit in will be critical. If getting pictures is really important you should sit as near to the activity as possible; although your subject may still be very small in your picture you will be able to have an enlargement made and crop out the irrelevant parts.

If you are in a crowd you must be careful with your framing. Because of the 'parallax' effect you may *see* an uninterrupted view through the viewfinder but *photograph* the top of the heads in front of you.

Some knowledge of the sport will help you choose the best position for taking pictures. At a school sports day, for example, the finish would be best for a sprint race, but for a hurdling race you would get better pictures standing by one of the flights as the young athletes clear them. Try to think about the best position before the race starts.

Get ready for the moment when movement is frozen – the 'peak of the action'. Press the shutter now and your picture will be sharp.

Opposite: an unusual angle can often increase the sense of speed in a sporting shot.

Panning is ideally suited to the autofocus camera. Focus on your subject and move smoothly with it, pressing the shutter as you go.

With many activities there is a point where the action is momentarily frozen – 'the peak of the action'. Press the shutter at this moment and you should get a sharp picture. But be careful not to do this during competitions; the click of a camera could destroy the competitor's concentration. These 'peaks' occur in many activities: high-jumpers across the bar; just before a football penalty kick; at the top of the tennis player's serve. By being ready for them you can compensate for slower shutter speeds.

A technique that is ideally suited to the autofocus camera is panning. You follow the activity in the viewfinder by moving your body. Because your movement compensates for that of the subject quite slow shutter speeds will produce sharp pictures. The key to successful panning is to maintain a smooth, even motion. You should press the shutter in the middle of the movement, making sure the autofocus frame marks are properly on the subject. Another result of panning is that, with the subject sharp, the background becomes blurred and enhances the feeling of speed in your picture.

Your choice of film will be very important for good action pictures. If you want to freeze the action, you will need an extra fast film (1000 ASA),

At local school or club sporting events you will be able to get a better, closer view than you would at a professional or national level.

If you position yourself so that the subject is moving towards you rather than straight across your field of vision, and therefore apparently moving more slowly, you will be more likely to get a clear picture.

especially in dull weather, but buy one with only 12 exposures: films of this speed are not ideal for normal family pictures. A 400 ASA film should be fast enough in bright weather.

Because of difficulties with position and lighting, indoor sports and activities pose even more problems. Unless you are very close it is pointless to use your flash; very few cameras have a flash with a greater range than 4 metres (13 feet). It will be better to rely on bright arena lights. Unless an event is being televised these lights will give a colour cast to your pictures; yellow with tungsten lights and green with mercury or sodium vapour. This cast can be corrected at the printing or enlarging stage with colour print film, but if you are using transparency film under tungsten lights you will need to use either a film suited to the lights or filters to correct the colour. Because filters cut down the light the special film is a better solution. It is very difficult to control the green cast of mercury or sodium vapour lighting using transparency material.

Both the Nikon L35AF and L135AF take film speeds up to 1000 ASA. The programmed shutter of the Nikon L35AF will use speeds of nearly 1/500th of a second in bright conditions or with fast film.

The space left in front of the cyclist increases the sense of movement here.

Gardens and nature

Your autofocus camera will give you wonderful general views of gardens and plants but, unless you use a close-up attachment, you will not be able to take pictures of individual flowers. There is often a temptation to get too close so if you are doing a lot of garden pictures it is worth carrying a length of string with you measured out to your minimum focusing distance.

Follow the instructions on page 50 for using close-up lenses. An added precaution when taking close-ups outside is to ensure that the flower is not moving in the wind. You can do this by making a windshield using white card which will also double as reflector.

You will get the best pictures on a hazy day when the sunshine is slightly diffused, so that shadows are not too black and contrasts not too strong. Backlight makes flowers look particularly attractive with the sun shining through their petals. You will not need to fill-in or use the backlight button in this situation.

If you are very concerned about getting the exact colour of flowers in your prints it will help to give the processor something as a reference to match it against. It might be necessary to order a special print for absolute fidelity.

Unless wild animals and birds are very tame you are unlikely to have much success photographing them because it will be difficult to get close enough. If you do manage to entice them very close by putting out food, try to take your pictures from a low viewpoint so that the animals don't look dwarfed.

At zoos you must be very careful with your focusing. There is always the danger that the bars or wire mesh of a cage will act as the point of focus. You might do better to use the focus lock to focus on something outside the enclosure at about the same distance away and then reframe your picture.

Try to get in close to tame birds while they are feeding.

You may find it easier to take pictures of slow-moving water birds.

Try to keep cage bars out of your zoo pictures and catch the animals while they are playing.

Work

The autofocus camera is ideal for anyone who needs record photographs as part of their work. Small enough to fit in a case or even your pocket, you can keep it with you at all times.

Some cameras are available with an added feature called a 'data back' which will automatically imprint either the date or the day and time onto the negative; it is invaluable when your pictures need to be identified by one of those factors. Data backs are incorporated in the cameras when they are made; they cannot be added at a later date.

A databack camera enables you to print the time or date on your picture. Leave a dark area in the bottom right-hand corner.

The covering power of the lens is ideally suitable for any pictures from building sites to production lines, but you will not be able to get close enough for detailed process pictures.

When you point your camera up to photograph a building your pictures will suffer from 'converging verticals', making the building appear an exaggerated wedge shape. The only way to cure this is to keep your camera level. You can do this by either moving further away, confining your subject to the top half of the viewfinder or finding a higher viewpoint.

Interior pictures are less easy because the flash range is limited, but it can be increased by 50% if you use a fast or extra fast film. However the real advantage of these films is that in most conditions you will be able to use the available light instead of flash. It is better to use a short roll of 12 exposures unless you know you have a lot of interior pictures to take.

Most industrial lighting will give a colour cast to your pictures and sodium vapour is one of the worst, giving a distinct green. Domestic lighting will give a yellow cast, but for room interiors the mixture of

If you photograph a building from directly below it will appear pointed. To rectify this move further away and position the building in the top half of your picture. You can then crop it down and enlarge.

daylight through the windows and ordinary tungsten room lighting will be quite acceptable. If colour accuracy is important you should warn the processor, but you may need to order handmade prints for complete accuracy. If you have used mixed lighting accurate colour correction is impossible.

If you need to take pictures on other people's property be sure to ask permission of the person in charge. You must also take care to wear the correct protective clothing for the environment.

If you are wearing eye protectors you may not be able to see the bright frame within the viewfinder. Keep the autofocus frame in the centre of the picture area as you see it and your focus and framing will be satisfactory.

The data imprinted on the negative is unlikely to have any legal standing but you can easily prove the earliest date on which a film or picture was taken by including that day's newspaper in the first picture on the film.

Night

As it gets dark there is no need to put away your camera: fast films and sophisticated exposure controls make it easy to take pictures at night. City centres, with their neon signs and floodlit buildings, are an obvious choice of subject, but bonfire parties and Christmas displays will also give you pleasing pictures.

To take cityscape pictures automatically you will need a reasonable number of bright lights; a small individual light in a sea of darkness will be badly over-exposed. With subjects you can get close to you should try to fill the viewfinder with the lit areas.

There is no point in using flash in these situations. The range of your flash is very limited and even if your subject is in range the flash light will kill the effect of the lights. You will get better effects from lights by using a star-burst filter which will turn the points into dramatic stars.

With fast or extra fast film you will be able to hand-hold the camera for most night shots, but with 100 ASA film or slower you will usually need to support it to get a clear picture. Large neon displays will be bright enough whatever film you are using (see page 122). Most city lighting is either neon, tungsten or sodium vapour which will give a colour cast, but in this context it enhances the picture; colour correction by film or processing can remove a lot of atmosphere.

The tallest buildings often have public galleries at the top from which you will get the best overall views, but you will usually be behind glass. Try to frame the picture you want with the camera against the glass because then you will have no problems with focusing or reflections. If not you can use your pocket tripod against a pillar for support, but you will have to focus first with the camera against the glass and use the focus lock or the self-timer. Be careful of reflections from the room and if necessary get someone to hold up a coat behind you.

Bright lights can confuse the focusing mechanism so you may have to focus on a darker area and reframe your picture; if possible check your

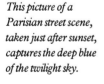

This picture of a Parisian street scene, taken just after sunset, captures the deep blue of the twilight sky.

I took this view of Tokyo through a fortieth floor window; and to avoid reflections in the glass I pulled a curtain behind me.

focus. Accurate focusing is very important with close subjects because everything in front and behind the point you are focusing on will be slightly blurred.

You will get better pictures at dusk when there is still some colour in the sky – the rich dark blue sky helps to reduce the contrast. Later in the evening you will get a very high contrast between the completely black sky and the bright lights.

A good bonfire will give off enough light to get good pictures with any film. The darkness of the sky may trigger your flash but it will be better not to use it as it will remove all the atmosphere. If you are photographing people try to get close so that you can see their faces clearly.

Fireworks and lightning will be difficult to photograph. The camera will have trouble focusing and you really need very long controlled exposures to get good results. If it is a really big display of fireworks it will be worth photographing any set pieces but individual fireworks are going to be disappointing. Lightning is so fast that by the time you have pressed the button it has gone. You might be lucky if you support the camera and take a number of pictures during the storm, but it is not really worth the effort.

Be particularly careful checking the quality of prints of your night shots. The contrast might confuse the automatic printers, resulting in washed out lights. Tell the processor that there are night shots on the film when you take it in.

In the home

There are treasured and valuable items in every home which are at risk from theft. If they should happen to be stolen it will help the police to trace them if you have a photographic record of them.

Your 35mm autofocus compact is not the ideal camera for this project; you may find it difficult to get close enough to small objects. You could use the close up lenses mentioned on page 50 but, unless the objects are tiny, an alternative would be to get an enlargement of the picture and cut out the relevant portion.

A photographic inventory of your valuables may help the police to trace them if they happen to be stolen.

You can use natural light for most pictures but it may be necessary to move things closer to a window or even outside.

Start by compiling a photo inventory to help your memory in the event of a break in. On a bright day put on all the room lights, stand in the middle and photograph each wall.

For small objects you can set up a little studio on a table in front of a window. To aid clarity arrange a plain background – a sheet of neutral coloured paper or thin card curved up behind the subjects.

A small sheet of white card propped upright on the room side of the window sill will reflect the light from the window and lighten the shadows, revealing more detail. When you have placed the subject against the background you can add a ruler to indicate scale.

To support the camera it is worth mounting it on a tripod or some other substantial base. This will allow you accurately to measure the minimum focusing distance to the subject. The camera may have trouble focusing on silver or very small objects, so hold a piece of neutral coloured card in front and to one side of the subject as a focusing substitute (see page 26).

It is difficult to photograph pictures in glass frames in artificial light,

You can use your camera to take a picture of the scene of an accident to accompany an insurance claim.

better to take them outside and position them so as to minimize any reflections.

When you get the prints back, write the dimensions and other details on the back and file them and the negatives in a safe place.

Carrying a camera with you in the car will enable you to record the details of any accidents you are involved in that may result in an insurance claim. Take pictures of the overall scene and of any particular damage so that you can give a comprehensive report.

Bad weather

Bad weather changes the quality of light so that everything takes on a different perspective. On overcast days, colours are muted and soft; after a rainstorm the light becomes unusually clear. There is absolutely no reason why you should put your camera away in weather like this. As long as you protect your camera and take care to use the right exposure you should be able to get some interesting pictures.

Try to protect your camera against wetness and extreme cold. A u/v filter over the lens will protect that from rain drops, and you should keep the camera inside your coat until you are ready to take the picture, giving the filter a careful wipe just beforehand. Don't load film in the wet but wait until you are sheltered. When you get back inside carefully wipe the camera with a dry cloth.

In snowy weather it is again a good idea to keep the u/v filter on, this

Don't put your camera away when it rains. You may catch some dramatic moments.

time to counteract the excessive blueness of the light. You should always keep the camera strap around your neck but particularly so in cold weather when cold fingers could easily drop it. Brush off any snow on the camera immediately because it is important it doesn't melt into the works, giving it a good wipe with a dry cloth or handkerchief when you get home.

To prevent condensation when you return indoors after taking pictures in the cold you should seal the camera into a plastic bag until it has warmed up. In cold weather batteries will lose their power more quickly and it is wise to keep a spare set in your pocket.

In strong winds it is very important to stand properly when taking pictures. Your camera will probably be using a slow speed and the buffeting of the wind makes it possible that you will spoil your pictures with camera shake.

Fog will obviously cause both autofocus and exposure problems. Set the ASA speed to half that of the film you have loaded and use a substitute subject to focus on.

On a dull day bright colours will appear even more brilliant.

In stormy weather the light can be uncannily clear.

Children's projects

As well as using the family camera to take snaps of your holidays and pets and friends, you may like to set yourself projects that will help you extend your skills as a photographer and, at the same time, discover more about the world around you.

Themes

One project you can set yourself is to be a collector. Give yourself a theme and then, whenever possible, try to take pictures to add to your collection. Your theme could be anything that interests you – uniforms, cars or even interesting signs. One photographer I know took pictures of any designs he saw using the rising sun motif, and eventually he made all the pictures into a book. Keep your project pictures in a special album with notes and background information. But it is important to try and make each picture more than just a record; it should work as a photograph as well.

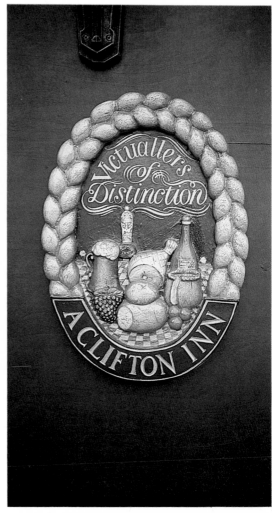

You could use your camera to make a collection – for example, of interesting signs.

Telling a story

You can use your camera to create picture stories like those in the magazines – either writing your own fictional story or making a documentary report. Whichever you choose, start by writing an outline, which is simply a few lines setting out your ideas or the plot.

If you are making up your story remember that you will have limited resources, so keep its setting and characters within reasonable bounds – you might find a pirate drama a little too expensive to stage!

If your story is a documentary you will need to do some advance research. 'A day in the life of . . . ' is a favourite theme, for example, and you should spend time with your subject before you write the outline. An alternative documentary project could be to photograph a series of people to show how they differ – your local shopkeepers and their shops would be interesting.

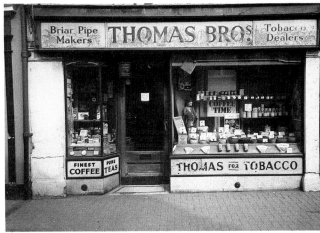

Or you might like to tell a story about your local High Street.

The next step is to make a storyboard to plan the picture you need, varying the shots so that you get detail as well as the broader view. You do not need to be able to draw well to do this because they need only be rough sketches. Now you are ready to start.

When you get your pictures back edit them carefully and then paste them in your album together with the words.

CHILDREN'S PROJECTS

Still life elements

There are four elements that make up any object in photographic terms: shape, texture, form and colour. Since photography is as much about seeing things as photographing them try to look at things in terms of these four elements.

Shape

Most of the information you get about something is in its shape. You can even recognise people and objects from silhouettes (see page 96) which give no other information. Shape applies both to individual items and to the way several objects look together.

Texture

Texture in your picture gives a feeling of reality. A photographic print is flat but texture in a picture gives a three-dimensional quality which is called depth. Texture is best brought out by side lighting.

Form

Form, like texture, is the illusion of shape created by light and shadow. Form is demonstrated by the way the light strikes the subject, so the position of the camera and the subject in relation to the light is important.

form *shape* *colour*

texture

Colour

Colour, or tone in black and white pictures, is the final element in identifying objects. If you are using colour film you can change colour using light or filters.

Still life

For many centuries still life has been one of the favourite subjects of painters, because it is a good way to experiment with composition and the effects of light. The best starting point is to look at still life paintings and photographs in magazines to see how other people have constructed them. Cut out examples you like and keep them in a scrapbook; you can also sketch your own ideas in the scrapbook.

Choose objects around the house for your first pictures and make some sketches of possible layouts – you don't have to be a good artist but the sketches will help you to make a good composition.

Because you are constructing the subject and the camera does not have to move you will find a tripod useful, as well as a +2 close-up lens; you may find the camera's inability to get close a disadvantage.

The thing to look for is the effect the light has on the shape and texture of your subjects. Front light on an orange simply makes it appear a flat, coloured disc: when you move the light to the side you begin to see the spherical shape and the texture of the skin. As you practise you will discover how you can get colours and shapes to balance each other in a pleasing composition. You can use artificial light or daylight and you will find that tracing paper and reflectors made from white card will be useful in controlling both the quality and direction of the light.

Use household objects to construct a still life making sketches first to work out the most pleasing composition.

Silhouettes

Until the invention of photography, silhouettes cut from black paper were a very popular way of doing portraits.

You can make silhouettes of anything but you might like to do portraits of your friends. You need enough information in your picture to identify your subject, so the profile view, showing the nose, chin and hair is the best to go for.

All you need as both background and light source is a big window on a bright day. If the view is clear sky so much the better, but if the window looks over the street or a garden you can tape tracing paper over it.

Turn the ASA/ISO dial of the camera to the next highest film speed, for example set 200 or 400 if you have 100 in the camera, and take the picture.

If you have used colour print you must tell the processor what you have done to get the best prints.

Enjoying your pictures

What happens at the printers

The first thing that happens when your film reaches the photographic laboratory is coding to make sure it gets back to you. Some photographic laboratories seal labels on to the film, others expose a code on to the last bit of film in the cassette. All the films of the same brand are then joined to make a long roll.

Colour negative films are developed in the C-41 process which consists of six stages. The developing machine has a tank containing a different chemical for each stage and the long roll of film is slowly drawn through them for the seventeen minutes the total process takes. Temperature is critical and is monitored electronically to ± 0.1°. Because the machine never stops, the chemicals are replenished continually throughout the day.

The developed roll of negatives is then loaded on to an automatic printer. At a rate of over 1000 prints an hour the printer first scans each negative to ascertain the correct colour and then makes the print. The prints are produced on a long roll of paper which is now processed in two chemicals for eight minutes.

At this stage some photographic laboratories will visually check the prints and order reprints for any that are below standard. The roll of prints is then automatically cut up, married to the correct negatives and packed for dispatch to you.

Reprints

Reprints are further prints made from one of your negatives after the first set of pictures. Because they have to be organised by hand they will cost more than en-prints and it is cheaper to take two pictures rather than ordering a reprint later.

If you need to order a reprint leave the negatives in their protective envelope and take them, together with the original print, to your photographic laboratory. It will be almost impossible to get a reprint that exactly matches the colours of the original.

Which service?

With continually changing prices and offers it is very difficult to decide what is value for money in photographic prints. Cheapest does not necessarily mean worst. The only rule is when you find a service that suits you should stay with it.

Mail order will be cheaper than a counter service, but complaining may involve you in a lengthy correspondence with a mail order laboratory. With a counter service you can look at your pictures before you leave and make comments then.

Negative care

Your negatives are both precious and easily damaged, so look after them carefully. There should be no need to handle them at all unless you are complaining about print quality (see overleaf). Keep them in the protective wallet they come in and store in a dry place. If you mark the subject of the pictures and the date on the outside of the wallet it will make finding them easier.

From left to right: film developing; printing; print developing; packaging.

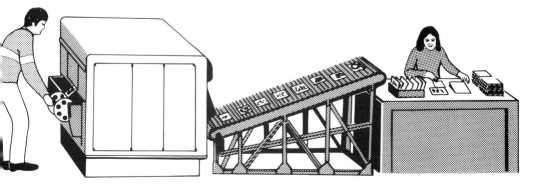

Print faults

Price competition in colour developing and printing has meant the introduction of automated machinery and a decline in quality checking. If you are disappointed by your results it is possible that the print is wrong. The following examples are intended to help you identify mistakes in the printing of your pictures.

Wrong colour

Different makes of colour film need different settings on the printing machines. If these are not changed you will get colour problems. If you have used coloured filters or artificial light for your pictures it will help if you tell the processor when you take in your film.

Colour cast

The printing machines are set to produce a print of average colour balance. If your negative has a predominance of one colour the machine will try to compensate by increasing the opposite colour. For example, if your subject is predominantly yellow, the machine will use too much blue.

The magenta cast is due to the amount of green in the background.

The large area of dark background has caused this figure to appear too light.

Flash and exposure

When you use flash it is likely that your picture will have a dark background. The machine will set an exposure averaged over the whole picture and your subject will be too light. Check the negative to see if there is detail in the face.

Drying and dust

If there are blotches and white spots on your original prints it is due to lack of care by the processor.

Lost film

With modern control systems it is unlikely that your film will be completely lost, but if it is and the pictures were important you may be entitled to compensation. You should consult your local consumer advice centre.

Mask cropping

A mask is used to hold the negative during printing. For stability this overlaps your picture by a small amount. This means that you will lose a little of your picture if your subject comes too close to the edges of the negative.

You will lose some of your picture in the printing if you frame it too tightly.

Enlargements

Although the prints you get from the processor are larger than the negatives, the term enlargement means reprinted pictures 7"×5" or bigger. You can order enlargements up to 24"×16".

There are two types of enlargements, machine and hand. Machine enlargements are much cheaper than those done by hand but they can have some of the failings in colour balance and quality that you find in en-prints. They are automatically made, using the whole negative, so you have no chance of being selective in the areas you want enlarged. With hand enlargements you can select the area of the picture you want enlarged and the quality will be much higher than machine enlargements; but the cost precludes it for all but your very best pictures.

Because of the price of enlargements be very critical of colour balance and how your instructions have been followed.

Cropping

All prints can be cut down to improve the composition or remove unwanted elements, but this applies particularly to enlargements. If you are ordering hand enlargements you should mark out the area you want on the en-print using a wax pencil. The processor will help you with the sizes that are available. It will be easier to work out your cropping if you make two L-shaped pieces of card that will let you experiment with different sizes.

You can also use them to experiment with any pictures you are going to cut down.

Showing your prints

Once your prints have been developed, it seems a pity to waste all your efforts by taking a quick look and then consigning them to the back of a drawer. If imaginatively displayed, they can give pleasure to all the family and brighten your home. The most popular method is to compile a family album, but enlargements are now so reasonably priced that you can easily use your pictures to make up an attractive wall display.

Firstly you should put the negatives away in a cool dry place. If they are properly looked after you will be able to get extra prints from them years later. The processor will have put them in a sleeve or envelope, and you should try not to touch them at all because they are very delicate and a scratch or thumb print will ruin them. Should you need to order reprints or enlargements it is better to take the whole set to the shop. Before filing the negatives, write the subject matter of the film clearly on the outside of the envelope.

It is unlikely that every picture on your film is perfect so before doing anything else you should reject any that do not come up to standard. Don't throw these away; unless they are really bad you can send them to friends or relations.

Tell the whole story of your holiday by including other mementoes in your album alongside your pictures.

Although all your prints will be the same size it will improve the appearance of your album if you vary the size of the pictures in it by cropping some. This will also help the composition by cutting out extraneous material. To give you some idea of the picture size you want before you cut it you can use two 'L' shaped pieces of cardboard to experiment. When you come to cut the picture use a very sharp craft knife

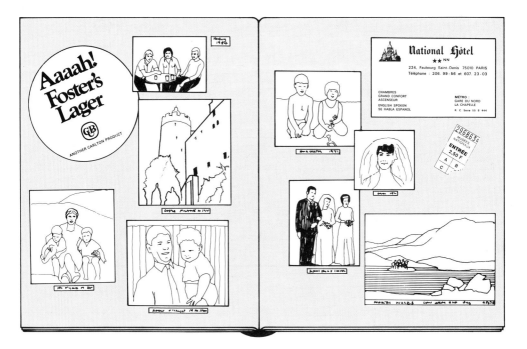

and a metal ruler, cutting on the outside of the ruler. Cropping will be easier if you choose the larger 7×5 prints that many processors offer these days.

Choose an album with big pages that will allow you more room for interesting layouts. Vary the layout from page to page and include other souvenirs like programmes, maps, holiday menus and postcards to add a different dimension.

Write, or better still type, captions for the pictures. If you do these on small labels, or separate pieces of paper for albums with adhesive pages, you can easily correct any mistakes.

There is a very wide range of picture frames available in the shops which can either be free standing or hung on the wall. It might be more interesting to buy the cheaper type and then add your own touches: a coat of bright paint or a fabric cover will give you a very individual display.

Many products are available for displaying pictures other than the traditional frames. Among the most popular are block mounts of wood or polystyrene. The wood mounts are available in a range of popular photographic sizes, and the polystyrene sheets are easily cut to suit your needs. Both are self-adhesive: you simply pull off a backing sheet and stick the picture down. You might brighten a blank wall by arranging a display with a single theme using different size pictures.

Use your prints to make attractive wall displays

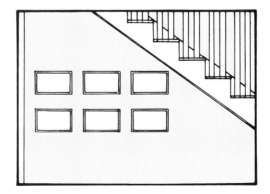

Showing your slides

It is easy to obtain prints from colour slides but the ideal way to display them is in the form of a slide show. The colours of a projected slide will be considerably brighter and truer than any colour print.

Always handle your slides with great care because they can easily get scratched or spoilt by finger marks. After editing it will be better to remount the best ones in more substantial glass-fronted mounts that will fully protect them from dirt and marks, in preference to the card or plastic type that the processors use.

The easiest way of showing slides is to use a simple battery-powered viewer. These are very economically priced but the slides must be fed individually by hand. There are more expensive mains-powered viewers that will take a preloaded magazine of slides and feed them automatically.

Caption your slides for future reference.

Viewers are handy to use but projectors will show off your slides to the best advantage.

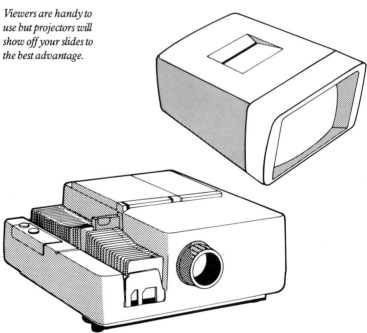

If you want to show your pictures to more than one or two people or you want to put a little production into the 'show', you will need a projector and screen. These are also available in a wide range of prices, from the simplest where you have to change the slides one at a time to more sophisticated ones which will change them at a predetermined rate or by remote control. At the top of the range are projectors that can be operated by a pre-recorded programme of instructions and sound track.

Slides are loaded into magazines for projecting. These magazines are available in circular or straight designs holding up to 100 slides, but they will not all fit every make of projector so be careful that you buy the right sort. The advantage of magazines is that you can leave the slides in them all the time.

Unless you have a convenient white wall you will need a screen for projecting. Screens come in two popular types – beaded and matt. Beaded screens, made from the same material as road signs, give a brilliant picture but need to be viewed from directly in front and are designed for large rooms. Matt screens can be viewed from the side as well and although the picture is not as bright as on a beaded surface they are cheaper and will be satisfactory in most situations.

The art of an interesting slide show is to edit your slides ruthlessly so that only the best or the relevant remain, and to put them in an interesting order. Remember that no slide should be on the screen for more than eight

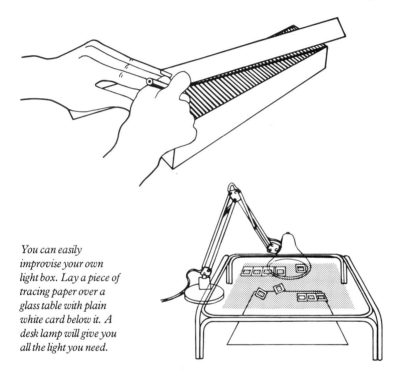

A diagonal line drawn across the top of an edited box of slides ensures that you keep them in the right order.

You can easily improvise your own light box. Lay a piece of tracing paper over a glass table with plain white card below it. A desk lamp will give you all the light you need.

seconds and the show should never be longer than fifteen minutes. It will be easier to do this if you can spread a set of slides out on a table and view them all at the same time. When professionals do this they use a purpose-built light box, but you can easily improvise one (see above). Spread out the slides, possibly from more than one film, and arrange them more or less in order. Then edit out any that are repeats or technically bad. The only excuse for including a less than perfect slide is if it is essential to your 'story'. It will help if you have a magnifying glass to help you look at the slides on your light box. Take your time over this stage and experiment with different running orders. Try to use slides of street or town names as 'titles' to punctuate the story. When you are happy with the order load them into a magazine and run it through a few times to make sure. In order to preserve the running order you should now mark or number the set.

You can add polish to your show if you make some notes that can act as a script or select some suitable music to play as background.

Pictures as greetings cards

There is a lot more you can do with your pictures than simply putting them into the album or making them into a slide show. Either commercially or with a little ingenuity you can use them to make a whole range of very personal greetings and gifts.

Christmas is the obvious occasion when it is nicer to send a greetings card that is personal to you and your family; it is, after all, the time you remake contact with distant friends. Most processors have special offers that include a greetings card made from your prints, but you can get simple cards cheaply printed at any 'instant print shop' and stick your prints on them. Either order reprints of your best family picture or, because children grow so fast, take a special family group in the autumn.

The birth of a new baby is an occasion when a picture of mother and child would be much more acceptable than a preprinted card. Again you can get the cards cheaply printed and stick the photograph on. Set up a picture when the mother and baby first come home; even if you have taken good pictures in the hospital they may be rather clinical.

A more practical use for your pictures is when you change address. If you send out pictures of the new house it will help friends to find you when they come to visit.

A family group in front of your new house makes an ideal change of address card.

It is much more economical simply to write your greeting or message on the back of your picture but you will need a special pen to do this. The paper used for modern photographs is plastic based and normal pens will not work.

Looking after your camera

Cleaning your camera

Your camera is a precision instrument; looking after it will give better pictures and years of reliable use. A dirty lens acts like a filter, cutting down the light, causing flare and reduced contrast. Dust and scraps of film inside the camera can cause marks on film and could lead to problems with the mechanism.

The equipment you need for cleaning a camera is very simple. A blower brush, a small paintbrush, lens cleaning tissue and fluid and a soft cloth are all you require, and they can be bought in a convenient pocket kit. Follow the sequence set out below, starting with the inside and ending with the lens. Keep the camera switched off while you clean it and keep the lens covered whenever possible. Treat all parts of the camera with great care while cleaning. *Don't lubricate your camera; and don't attempt to repair it if anything goes wrong – take it back to your dealer.*

Stage one – the inside

1. First check that the camera is empty. Many priceless pictures have been ruined by inadvertently opening the back of a loaded camera. You can easily do this by looking at the film identification window and the frame counter.

2. Blow any dust or film scraps out with the blow brush. Although film scraps are not a frequent problem with an autowinding camera small pieces can sometimes break off from the sprocket holes.

3. Use the paint brush gently to clean the channels where the camera back seals.

Stage two – the body

1. Use the blower brush or the paintbrush on the main bodywork, remembering especially to clean the rear viewfinder window.

2. Use the cloth gently to clean the autofocus, viewfinder and exposure metering windows and the front of the flash.

Stage three – the lens

The lens, like the windscreen of a car, needs to be clean to work efficiently.

1. First use the blower brush to puff away any dust or grit.

2. Then fold a sheet of lens tissue to a small square and clean the lens with a corner using a clockwise motion. If the lens is particularly dirty you should use a drop of lens cleaning fluid *on the tissue. Do not put fluid directly on the lens and do not use fluid specially designed for the cleaning of spectacles.* If you now gently breathe on the lens you will see if it is clean by the evenness of the condensation. Replace or close the lens cover.

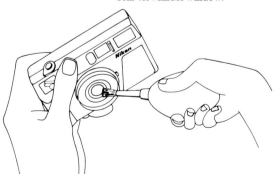 

A convenient Nikon camera care kit is available from dealers.

Batteries

All the automatic functions of your camera are powered by batteries and it will not work without them or when they are very weak. Most cameras use two 1.5v batteries of the AA size. There are several types of these on the market but it is better to use the manganese-alkaline type as opposed to zinc carbon; they are more expensive but last longer and are sealed to prevent leakage. One of the big advantages of 1.5v AA batteries is world-wide availability.

Do not use rechargeable nickel cadmium (Ni-Cad) batteries in your camera. They do not give the 1.5 volt output needed for peak performance.

Because batteries gradually lose power it is advisable to change them once a year, however often you have used the camera. For the same reason buy them from a shop with a rapid turnover.

When loading new batteries make sure you get the polarities right or you risk damaging your camera.

When you change batteries replace both of them and do not mix different types. After you have replaced the batteries check them by putting a half-pressure on the button to see if the camera will focus.

If you do not use your flash, a set of batteries should last for about twenty films, but frequent use of flash will reduce this dramatically to around five films.

Before you replace the batteries you should clean both the camera and the battery terminals to ensure that you have a good connection. Briskly rub the battery terminals on rough cloth, or use the eraser on the end of a pencil. The ends of the batteries are marked with +/− which indicates their polarity. These markings are also in the battery compartment and you must check that you have them the right way round.

Data backs use different batteries that are less easily obtained than the AA types.

The Nikon L35AF and L135AF use two 1.5v batteries. The L35AD also uses two LR-44 or SR-44 type batteries in the data back. The L35AF has an on/off switch; the switch for the L135AF is incorporated in the lens cover.

Protecting your camera and film

Insurance and crime prevention

However much care you take of your camera there is always the risk of accidental damage or theft. Most cameras have a serial number, in many cases on the base, and you should take a note of this. Make sure that your camera is insured, preferably by adding it to an 'all risk' policy. You should check that the insurance cover will also apply to overseas travel.

To protect your camera from theft, or at least to help its recovery if this happens, the police recommend that you mark it with your postcode and house number. There are various methods of doing this of which the most efficient is scratching the postcode on the base plate with a scriber.

In the car

If you keep your camera in your car try not to let it get too hot. Heat is particularly bad for film and could spoil the one in the camera including any pictures you have already taken.

Back shelves and glove compartments are the worst offenders because, in sunny weather, they can get very hot. Placing your camera in view is also an invitation to theft. If you need to keep your camera in the car the floor behind the front seats will be best, but keep it in its case to protect it.

On holiday

If you are travelling by air your hand baggage will be inspected using an x-ray machine. These x-rays can damage your film, particularly if you are using one with a high ASA speed (a fast film). It is better to keep your camera round your neck and any spare film in your pockets. If you are stopped, request a hand-check of your camera and any film. X-rays will not harm the camera itself.

If you take the camera on the beach keep it in a bag. This will keep it away from the sand and provide some cooling shade. If it gets splashed with salt water wipe it carefully with a damp cloth to remove any salt, and dry it afterwards with a soft cloth. Rain is less of a problem and you should simply dry the camera by gently wiping it with a soft cloth.

An ultraviolet filter can be kept on the lens to protect it from water, sand and dust without affecting your pictures.

General

Keep your camera in its case or with the lens cap on whenever you are not using it. The lens is particularly vulnerable to scratches. Probably you will want to use your camera all year round but, if you do need to store it, choose a cool, dry place. Take out the batteries, which you should keep in a fridge or freezer to preserve their power. Because the image on your film will slowly deteriorate from the moment it is taken you should not store your camera with film left in it. It is better to finish the film and have it processed. You can safely keep any unused film in the freezer with the batteries as long as you allow it to defrost for an hour and a half before loading it.

What went wrong?

Picture faults

This guide is intended to help you identify and correct any problems in technique or camera handling that are resulting in unsatisfactory pictures.

Transparency film is simply processed and returned to you without any secondary process. This means that if your colour slides are disappointing the problems are probably with your technique. This is not necessarily the case with colour prints. Colour printing is a secondary process and what you think are your faults may simply be poor quality prints. Check the section on print faults (page 98) first.

Over-exposure

It is most likely that you have set too low an ASA speed on the camera; check each time you load a film that it is set correctly. With very fast films (1000 ASA) the light may simply have been too bright for the film (see page 22).

Negative film The print is murky with little contrast and the negative very dense.

Transparency film The picture is too light.

Under-exposure

It is likely that you have set too high an ASA speed on the camera; check each time you load a film that it is set correctly. If there was not enough light for a satisfactory picture the camera's low light warning should have been heeded and flash used (see page 22).

Negative film The print is lacking detail with a muddy look and the negative is very pale.

Transparency film The picture is too dark.

Correct exposure

Fogged film If this occurs at the beginning of the film it would indicate that the film was loaded in bright sunlight. If it occurs in the middle of the film it means that the back of the camera has been inadvertently opened, exposing the film to random light.

Wrong film Because the light from domestic bulbs is more yellow than daylight, pictures taken in it will appear yellow. This can be corrected to some extent when printing colour negative film but with transparency film you should use an 80A filter or a film balanced for tungsten light (see page 14).

Wrong focusing (composition) Groups with a gap in them or small subjects will not activate the focus mechanism. You should focus on a substitute object approximately the same distance away and use the focus lock to hold that while you frame your picture (see page 26).

Wrong focusing (glass) If you stand square on to glass the autofocus mechanism will focus on it. You should press the camera against the glass or stand at an angle to the glass (see page 26).

Picture blur If the whole picture is blurred the speed selected by the camera was too slow for hand-holding. This will normally happen in poor light and you should use a tripod or support; change to a faster film; or use flash when the light is bad (see pages 15, 20, 22).

Subject blur If fast moving subjects appear blurred the speed selected by the camera was too slow. You should use faster film for action subjects, especially in dull weather (see page 15).

Framing Because the lens and the viewfinder are separate you must compensate with subjects closer than 2 metres (6½ feet) (see page 24).

Obstruction You must take care that your fingers or the strap do not obstruct the lens when you are taking the picture (see page 20).

Flare This occurs when direct light, usually from the sun, comes into the picture. When you are taking a picture towards the sun you should try to use your hand to shade the lens, or change your viewpoint.

Your shadow When taking pictures on a sunny day with the sun behind you, you must take care not to get your own shadow in the picture. Move to one side or raise the camera.

Too small When you know the subject you often forget how small they will appear in the finished print if you are too far away. When photographing people it is better to fill the viewfinder.

Slanting horizon
The camera was not held straight when you took the picture. You may have pushed down too hard when you pressed the shutter. Always check the background before taking the picture.

118

Too far The subject was too far away from the camera. Remember that small flash units have a range of around 3 metres (10 feet) with 100 ASA film and 4 metres (13 feet) with 400 ASA film. Check that you have not set too high an ASA speed on the camera. Get closer to your subject. This fault will appear worse with transparency film. You could get the same effect if your fingers were obstructing the flash. (see page 44).

Fall off The light from a flash loses strength with increased distance, which makes it impossible to light a spread-out subject properly. Try to arrange your subjects parallel to the camera (see page 44).

Reflections If you take your picture square on to glass, mirrors or any shiny surface, they will reflect the light from your flash. Try to avoid these surfaces in your picture but if this is not possible stand at an angle of about 45°. Get spectacle wearers to turn their faces slightly (see page 44).

Camera faults

Although your camera has been designed for ease of operation, there may be times when you experience some difficulties in operating it. This check list is intended to help you quickly identify and rectify any problems.

The shutter release button cannot be depressed.

The problem is most likely to be the batteries; but make sure first that the camera is switched on. Take out the batteries and clean the contacts on a piece of rough cloth. When you replace them check that you have the polarity correct.

Try again. If the problem persists you should replace the batteries with new ones. The long-life manganese alkaline type are best and you should not use rechargeable NiCad batteries.

The film will not advance to the next frame.

Make sure that the film is properly loaded (see page 18). Check the batteries as above and replace them if necessary.

The motor stops while the film is rewinding.

This will also be because the batteries are run down.

The flash takes a long time to charge and the camera seems sluggish.

Either the batteries are running down or you have loaded the wrong type. Replace them with manganese alkaline type.

The batteries run out of power quickly.

If you are using the flash frequently manganese alkaline batteries should last for about five films and for twenty without flash. Check that you are not leaving the flash on for long periods and that you are switching the camera off when not in use.

The flash pops up in bright situations.

This will happen if you obstruct the exposure metering window with your finger, so check that you are holding the camera correctly.

If these simple remedies do not work you should take the camera to a qualified dealer.
DO NOT ATTEMPT ANY CAMERA REPAIRS YOURSELF. RETURN IT TO YOUR RETAILER. YOU MAY DAMAGE THE CAMERA AND INVALIDATE YOUR GUARANTEE.

Endings

Problem lighting

There are occasions when you are taking pictures indoors or at night and cannot use flash. To get a good picture in these situations you need to take special care, and this guide is intended to help you choose a suitable film and technique. The brightness of individual light sources vary and the recommendations below are based on average available light with the subject filling the viewfinder.

Most cameras indicate the need to use flash at the same light level irrespective of the speed of film you are using. Some cameras simply indicate flash should be used whilst others automatically activate it when the light is low. In the latter case, simply hold or tape the flash down to suppress it.

All artificial lights will give a colour cast that can be reduced on colour prints.

Bright home interiors at night

100 ASA: Not really suitable.
400 ASA: Suitable but you need to support the camera.
1000 ASA: Suitable. Colour cast as above.

Bright home interiors in daylight

100 ASA: Suitable but not for fast-moving subjects.
400 ASA: Suitable.
1000 ASA: Suitable.

Bright city street scenes

100 ASA: Possible if you support the camera.
400 ASA: Suitable.
1000 ASA: Suitable.

Neon signs

100 ASA: Suitable.
400 ASA: Suitable.
1000 ASA: Suitable.

Bright shop windows

100 ASA: Suitable but hold the camera firmly.
400 ASA: Suitable.
1000 ASA: Suitable.

Floodlit buildings

100 ASA: Not really suitable but possible if you support your camera.
400 ASA: Suitable but support the camera.
1000 ASA: Suitable.

Fairs and illuminations

100 ASA: Suitable but the camera must be supported.
400 ASA: Suitable but you must hold the camera correctly, preferably bracing yourself.
1000 ASA: Suitable.

Indoor and floodlit outdoor sports

100 ASA: Not really suitable but possible if you hold the camera correctly. Not for moving subjects.
400 ASA: Suitable but not for moving subjects.
1000 ASA: Suitable including some moving subjects with panning technique (see page 80).

Swimming pools (artificial light)

100 ASA: Not suitable unless very bright.
400 ASA: Suitable but not for moving subjects.
1000 ASA: Suitable, possibly including moving subjects.

Churches, galleries and museums

100 ASA: Not suitable.
400 ASA: Suitable but the camera will need to be supported.
1000 ASA: Suitable but the camera will need to be held correctly.

Amateur dramatics

100 ASA: Not suitable.
400 ASA: Not really suitable and camera will need supporting.
1000 ASA: Suitable but not for moving subjects.

Fireworks, lightning and moonlight

These subjects are not really suitable for your camera although you might get some results with fast or extra fast film.

Technical terms

aperture The size of opening set by the camera to control the amount of light reaching the film through the lens. Used in conjunction with the **shutter speed** to give you an accurate **exposure**.

artificial light Any light other than **daylight**. This can include your flash or ordinary household lights.

ASA (American Standards Association). This is the most popular means of measuring a film's sensitivity to light. The higher the ASA speed, the more sensitive or faster the film is. Some makers are replacing it with the identical **ISO** numbers.

autofocus A system where your camera measures the distance to your subject and focuses the **lens** accordingly.

available light The existing light available for you to take your pictures without using flash. It could mean daylight, floodlights or domestic lights.

backlight When the light is coming towards you from behind the subject.

backlight compensation With your subject in shadow you expose for the shadow as opposed to the brighter light behind.

background The part of your picture behind the subject.

cassette The light tight container that holds 12, 24 or 36 exposures of 35mm **film**. When the film has been used it must be rewound into the cassette.

close-up A picture taken closer than the normal minimum of your camera.

close-up lens A supplementary lens that screws onto your camera to enable you to take close-up pictures.

colour negative film The film you use when you want to get prints of your pictures.

colour transparency film The film you use when you want projection slides of your pictures.

cool Any light or colour that tends towards blue.

composition The arrangement of your subject in the viewfinder to make a more attractive picture.

contrast A comparison between the lightest and the darkest parts of your picture. High contrast is a great range and low contrast is a narrow range.

cropping Cutting a print down in size to improve its composition.

DIN The German standard of film sensitivity. Less common than **ASA**.

daylight film Film designed to use in daylight or with your flash.

diffused light The even, shadowless light that you get in overcast weather.

emulsion The light-sensitive part of the **film** or **print**. Colour film is made of three layers of emulsion.

enlargement Commonly used to denote a print larger than the original received from the photographic laboratory.

en-print Popular 5″×3½″ size of print from a 35mm **negative**.

exposure Taking the picture by letting a controlled amount of light (**aperture**) reach the film, through the lens, for a controlled amount of time (**shutter speed**).

fast film Film with an **ASA** speed of 400 or more used for pictures in poor light or of fast-moving subjects. Fast film will appear grainier than **slow film**.

fill-in Using your flash or a reflector in daylight to brighten up dark shadows on your subject.

film frame counter A numbered disc on your camera that tells you how many pictures you have taken on a film.

film speed The sensitivity of film to light. The film speed is normally measured in **ASA, ISO** or **DIN** numbers. Higher numbers are more sensitive to light.

filter Anything transparent put in front of the lens to change the picture. Filters can give you special effects, changes in colour and many more creative results.

flare The result of unwanted direct light shining in your lens.

flash Commonly means an electronic flash that produces a very bright light by passing a burst of electricity through a glass tube. You should get several thousand flashes from a tube.

foreground The part of your picture in front of the subject.

grain The visible structure of a film. You will get more grain with a faster film. *See* **fast film**.

highlights The brightest areas of your picture.

infinity The furthest point your camera will focus on for distant shots.

ISO (International Standards Organisation). Identical to ASA as a measure of film's sensitivity to light and slowly replacing it. *See* **ASA**.

LED (light-emitting diode). A light in your viewfinder giving you information.

lens The optical device used to concentrate and focus your picture on the film.

medium film Film with a speed between 100 and 200 ASA used for most pictures in most lights.

natural light Sunlight.

negative A reverse image of the picture you took. Produced by negative film from which you get **prints** and **enlargements**.

over-exposure A very light picture caused by too much exposure.

panning Taking a picture while swinging your camera to follow a fast-moving subject so it will be sharp.

parallax error When you cut off part of a close subject because you did not allow for the lens and viewfinder being separate.

programme Automatic exposure measurement when the camera gives you the best average combination of aperture and shutter speed.

reflector Any light-coloured material used to throw light back onto the subject to lighten the shadows.

reprint A print you order after the film is processed. Usually more expensive than the original.

reversal film Another name for **colour transparency film**.

self-timer A device on the camera that delays the picture being taken by approximately ten seconds. It allows you to appear in your own pictures.

shutter The device behind the lens that keeps light away from the film until you take the picture, opening for a controlled time to admit light when you press the release.

shutter speed The fraction of time the shutter remains open to make the picture. Used in conjunction with the **aperture** to control the **exposure**.

slide The translucent picture you get from a **colour transparency film**. You have to use a projector or a viewer to see it to its best advantage.

slow film A film with an ASA of less than 50 which will give fine-grain results but must be used in bright light.

sprocket holes The small rectangular holes along both sides of the film used to transport it accurately through your camera.

transparency *See* **slide**.

tripod A three-legged camera support giving greater stability than can be achieved by hand-holding. Vital for long exposures.

tungsten film Colour transparency film designed for use in tungsten light.

tungsten light The light given by household or photographic light bulbs.

under-exposure A dark image caused by insufficient light reaching the film.

viewfinder The part of the camera you look through to frame your picture. It can also provide focusing and battery life information.

warm Any light that tends towards red/orange/yellow.

winder The mechanism built in to the camera that winds on the film and recocks the shutter after each shot. Some also rewind the film when it is finished.

Index

Acknowledgements

I would like to express my sincere thanks to Anne Conway, Les Mehan, Fanny Dubes and Terry Hewett for all their efforts in taking pictures for me.

To Harry Collins, Peter Bonnington, John Slater and Charlotte Beer of Nikon (UK) Ltd for all the help they gave me with cameras and technical information, Mike Holmes of Introphoto for the loan of the filters and Peter at West 8 colour lab.

Finally and especially to Hilary Davies of Pan Books for being a super editor.

PICTURE CREDITS

Anne Conway
pp 33; 37 (top); 41 (bottom); 42 (right); 45 (centre); 48; 54 (both); 55; 60; 65 (left); 67; 83 (bottom); 86; 90; 91 (top); 94 (all except bottom left).

Fanny Dubes
pp 2; 17 (top); 41 (top right); 57; 58 (left); 69; 80 (bottom); 102; 103.

Terry Hewett
pp 6 (bottom); 15 (right); 17 (bottom); 25 (both); 26 (both); 42 (left); 56 (both); 59; 61; 62 (both); 63; 64; 80 (top); 81 (top); 89.

Les Meehan
pp 14; 49 (bottom); 50 (all); 51; 65 (right); 68 (top); 76 (centre); 79; 82; 88; 91 (bottom); 92 (both); 93 (both); 95.

Geoffrey Mulligan
pp 70; 77 (top).

Brian Mumford
pp 8 (top); 15 (left); 46 (both); 58 (bottom); 66; 78; 83 (top).

John Slater
pp 28 (both); 32; 35 (bottom); 37 (bottom); 47; 72.

All other photography by **Joe Partridge.**